THAT
MOMENT
WHEN...

THAT MOMENT WHEN...

Life Stories from Way Back Then

MO GILLIGAN

EBURY
SPOTLIGHT

1 3 5 7 9 10 8 6 4 2

Ebury Spotlight, an imprint of Ebury Publishing
20 Vauxhall Bridge Road
London SW1V 2SA

Ebury Spotlight is part of the Penguin Random House group of companies
whose addresses can be found at global.penguinrandomhouse.com

Copyright © Momo G Limited 2021

Mo Gilligan has asserted his right to be identified as the author of this Work
in accordance with the Copyright, Designs and Patents Act 1988

The publisher and author have made every effort to credit the copyright
owners of any material that appears within, and will correct any
omissions in subsequent editions if notified.

First published by Ebury Spotlight in 2021

www.penguin.co.uk

A CIP catalogue record for this book is available from the British Library

ISBN 9781529109207

Printed and bound in Great Britain by Clays Ltd, Elcograf S.p.A.
Imported into the EEA by Penguin Random House Ireland,
Morrison Chambers, 32 Nassau Street, Dublin D02 YH68.

Penguin Random House is committed to a sustainable future for
our business, our readers and our planet. This book is made from
Forest Stewardship Council® certified paper.

To everyone who has supported me on
this incredible journey so far.
Thank you …
You've changed my life.

LONDON BOROUGH OF RICHMOND UPON THAMES DISCARDED	
90710 000 485 641 FROM	
Askews & Holts	08-Sep-2021
B GIL	
RTH	

This book is a work of non-fiction based on the life, experiences and recollections of the author. In some cases names of people have been changed to protect the privacy of others.

Contents

INTRODUCTION

The Grind Before the Grind

Who's this Mo Gilligan guy, then?

It's a good question, a fair question – and, if you have read anything about me in a newspaper or online over the last two years or so, you probably think you know the answer. There has been a history of me and my life put out there, and it runs roughly like this:

> *Young Black comedian. Grew up in south London.*
> *Worked in Levi's. Did the 'Coupla Cans' video online.*
> *Drake shouted him out and made him famous. Did some*
> *live comedy and went on television. The end.*

Well, that's a great story for a Hollywood film, but the truth is that it hasn't really been like that. Or, rather, it hasn't been *quite* like that. There has been a whole lot more going on in my life than just that.

Life is all about moments. Or Mo-ments! Mo-ments when … things happen. But things don't just happen of their own accord. You have to work hard at them. You have to grind away in order to become successful. Well, this book is the story of my grind.

Or rather, again, it's more than that. It's the story of the grind *before* the grind.

That Moment When ... is the story of how Mosiah Gilligan turned into Mo the Comedian, then turned into Mo Gilligan. It's about the me that existed before I started doing comedy, as well as after. And it's about the different sides of me that people probably don't know about.

Let me try to put it in food terms ...

My true story has got lost in media coverage, a bit like the dumpling in a bowl of the soup you get from a Caribbean take-away. You know the feeling when you're poking around in the Styrofoam cup looking for it? You're like, *Woah! Where's the dumpling gone?*

Well, this book is like finding that last dumpling in the oxtail soup when you think they've all gone.

That Moment When ... pulls out those hidden dumplings from my life. It fills in the story that people think they know. It says, 'Yeah, I worked in retail, and what's wrong with that? There are thousands of people doing that every day – big shout out to them!'

Because I *was* working in retail, yeah, but I was also hustling like mad to get my comedy career started. I was telling jokes at weddings, running my own comedy night, and travelling up and down the country to perform at shows when I couldn't even afford my train fare home.

This is the story of where I came from, how I began, the good gigs that I played – and the ones that didn't go so well. The things I did right and the mistakes I made. It's about the

Mo-ments that got me from where I started to where I am now: from being that young Black kid on a south London council estate to going viral with 'Coupla Cans', fronting *The Lateish Show*, joining *The Masked Singer* and, as I write this, having just sold out my first show at the O2.

Rah! How did all *that* happen to this Mo Gilligan fella? Well, this book explains it all … and it starts in a time where the most important things in my life, after my family, were my friends and an adventure playground.

1

THAT MOMENT WHEN ...

Life Is All About Playing Out

When you're a kid, your world is small and you know it off by heart. Life is defined by those small moments you share with your mates on the block, on the estate and down the road. You're a little community and your friends are the only guys that matter. It's a time of freedom.

I sometimes think we spend our adulthoods trying to get that freedom back. It was so pure and good-spirited. When you're a kid, school might be shit, yeah, but everything else is fun. Playing is everything, fun is the only thing that matters ... and the most fun of all is *playing out*.

Playing out is what you live for as a kid. As an adult, you live for going to festivals and on holidays, or going raving with your mates. But when you're a kid, the summer holidays are the best thing because you get to play out for six weeks. *Everybody – playing out for six weeks! Man, it felt like it went on forever! It felt like six months! It was just the best time.*

The crucial thing you needed to play out was a bike. We thought about bikes like kids think about consoles today. Nobody really had consoles as they were so expensive. It was all about having a bike. If you got a bike, it wouldn't be a new one. It would have been passed down to you by a brother or cousin. Off you'd go, to the park and down to the woods. Sometimes, you didn't even know where you were going. You and your mates would cycle for hours. You'd get lost and take ages to find your way home. Sometimes, your parents wouldn't even notice you'd gone. Other times, they'd be worried sick: 'Where the hell have you been?'

And then you'd be in trouble. Big time.

We'd cycle to Dulwich Park, which wasn't all that far, and have a mad-fun day. We'd have no money at all: or, if we were lucky, someone might have 50p and we'd spend it on ice poles or onion rings. The taste of the summer, man!

If your bike ever broke, you had to figure out how to fix it yourself. *Shit, how could we be fixing bikes? We were just little kids!*

If you wanted to play out on your bike, you'd have to make sure everyone else had their bike as well. *Who wants to ride on their own?* We had skateboards, as well, but not cool skateboards – they were just like wide, flat, round planks of wood on wheels.

I grew up in Denmark Hill, south London. It was our playground. We'd go to the top of one of the hills around our estate and skateboard back down. Cars would be coming around the corner and we would be zooming straight towards them at 20mph. Our only brakes were our feet.

Thinking back, I can't believe how dangerous it was!

• • •

My mum raised me and my two older sisters. They were eight years and seven years older than me, so when I was six, they were already teenagers. It made them seem ancient: *Woah! My sisters are so OLD!*

The cool thing about having older sisters was that they were connected to pop culture and music. It was through them that I knew about the likes of Usher, Mary J. Blige and Jodeci because they had big posters of them in their rooms. It was also because of them that I was introduced to R&B, hip-hop and old-school garage, which I heard booming through the walls separating our bedrooms.

Because my sisters were so much older, I was definitely the baby of the family. I still am, really. Even today, I will go to my mum's house and my sisters will be there. As soon as I walk in the door, Mum will say:

'Ah, Mo! Would you like something to eat?'

And my sisters will say, 'What?! We've been here for two hours now and you haven't even offered us a drink!'

But, as a kid, having older sisters was cool. Maybe they can't protect you from playground bullies like older brothers can, but I learnt stuff from them. It was down to them that I knew anything about grooming growing up. I saw them getting into make-up and would watch them creaming their skin or putting stuff in their hair: *Oh, OK, you put* that *in your hair and* that's *what it does to it!*

•　•　•

My parents separated when I was very young, which meant I spent a lot of weekends at my dad's house in Brixton. I also spent those weekends with my other sister on my dad's side of the family.

Dad was a Rastafarian from St. Lucia, over six foot tall, with long dreads that he used to tie up underneath his hat. Most of the time he'd dress in full-on camouflage: military gear with the combat boots and everything. He'd wear it with his Haile Selassie medals, singing songs as he walked down Brixton High Street.

My dad would take me and my half-sister to Notting Hill Carnival. We'd hold each other's hands and walk and walk for hours. Today, I know that Notting Hill Carnival is pretty cool, but when you are seven or eight ... *man, it was boring ...*

Watching older people having fun! Who cares about that?

Dad was vegan, like a lot of Rastas. I remember being with him one time and asking, 'Dad, can I have some jerk chicken?' He was like, 'No, Mo, you're not eating chicken! I'll get you a vegetable patty ... '

My dad would get me stuff, though – sweets, or shoes, or even just posters that were for sale on the floor outside Brixton Tube station. Rap gods like 2Pac, Arsenal posters, stuff like that. He didn't live with us – but he was very much part of my life.

• • •

When you went to play out, the first thing you did was knock for your friends. You'd go round all your friends' houses, one by one, to ask their mums if they could come out. I used to always do them in exactly the same order.

First, we'd go to my best friend Adam's house. Adam *always* came out. Then we'd go call for Little Michael. He wasn't always allowed out. It would be about fifty-fifty. Little Michael lived in the same block as Greg and Luke, two brothers that also played out with us. Greg was two or three years older than us and, because of that, I always believed every single word he said. It's funny, at that age, you believe everything that older kids tell you. Age gaps are a big thing when you're a kid.

Another boy who was a bit older – maybe he was eleven when I was nine – was a kid called James who lived with his dad, granddad and a little bulldog. He was one of the lucky guys who had a console: a PlayStation. Man, I loved playing *Tekken*!

James was a proper pyromaniac. He loved setting fire to stuff. He even smoked, at the age of only eleven. He was the original fire starter.

James had an edge and kids love that. James was tight with a boy who lived down the road called Danny. If James was bad, Danny was *bad* bad. He would set more fires than James!

I wasn't bad, or *bad* bad, like that. I spent most of my time with Adam and Little Michael. Michael was – guess what? – little, but not tiny. We only called him that to differentiate him from another kid called Michael who lived in the next block.

That Michael was proper crazy. He was the kid that would run around on top of walls and do backflips. We would all have our mouths hanging open watching him, and urging him on:

'Wow! Do that again!'

Michael thought he was a super Saiyan! He would tell us, 'You lot try and fight me, right? I won't fight back!'

'Eh?' we would ask him. 'What?'

'Hit me! I won't hit you back!'

Brother, we were throwing everything at this guy! But nothing landed. He dodged everything like a little Black Bruce Lee.

There were these low garages on our estate, and we would all be jumping off the roofs and fly-kicking Michael on the way down! He would go flying to avoid every blow ... then bounce straight back up again.

'Go on! Fight me again!'

It was so mad. Maybe he *was* a super Saiyan, in the body of a ten-year-old south London boy.

Michael loved kung fu but he was also a proper geek. When we were play fighting, he would do this weird, scary thing where he'd suddenly say:

'Oh! I'm malfunctioning!'

'What?'

And then he would pretend to turn into RoboCop, 'Oh, I'm malfunctioning!' Then he'd start doing all these backflips.

We only ever play-fought with Michael. You wouldn't want to get into a real fight with him: he might have been a geek, but he could still hold his own – that, and he owned his own pair of nunchakus.

Even Michael's mum was cool. Sometimes she'd give us bread. Random, right? She'd just hand us slices of warm bread in tissue like we were a gang of Victorian street urchins.

For me, Michael was one of the coolest kids on the estate, because he showed us that it was OK to be yourself. You didn't have to follow the crowd and you didn't have to be a James or Danny by setting fire to stuff. It was alright to be different.

I don't know where he is now, but knowing Michael he probably invested early in Bitcoin, or is out there working on his flux capacitator. I hope he's doing well for himself.

• • •

If I was lucky, my sisters might take me to the pictures on a Saturday. They took me and Adam to see *Space Jam* when I was eight. That movie was a big deal at the time – *Looney Tunes* had a moment in the 1990s when everyone was wearing Iceberg tops with the characters on them. People were even naming their tags after them.

We went to Peckham Cinema where they had a special deal with McDonald's over the road, which meant that after the movie we could go and have a Big Mac and fries for £1.99 or something.

That's a seriously cool day when you're eight years old.

I couldn't always play out at weekends, though, because if I wasn't at my dad's eating tofu, then I'd be with my mum going shopping at the markets. We'd go to *all* the markets. Brixton Market, Vauxhall Market, sometimes we'd even go to Wembley Market.

First, she'd go to the butcher and then she'd go to the fishmonger. But she wasn't just going in to get these things, she was *haggling*.

'How much is that fish?' she'd ask. 'Five pounds? But you did it for me for four pounds last week! Can you descale it, cut the head and tail off, weigh it again and do it for four pounds?'

Those markets were mad. There would be flies sitting all over the meat and fish. There would *literally* be a fly sitting on a fish's eyeball.

We'd walk around the markets where I'd see slaughtered chickens hanging from hooks above our heads and goat heads sitting on tables, looking like a scene from *Saw*. There would be weird fish you'd never seen before, like parrot fish, and I'd think, *Who the hell will buy that?* But people did.

As we walked around the market, inevitably my mum would bump into one of her friends and start talking to them. I hated that because they could go on for *hours*! We'd be there in the middle of the market with her tartan trolley on wheels and a blue carrier bag full of meat while Mum was talking away like there was no tomorrow.

Meanwhile, I'd be looking over my shoulder, praying I wouldn't be spotted by any of my classmates. That was the worst – when you ran into a kid from school who was basically doing what you were doing.

He's got a bag of meat, I've got a bag of meat. He's got a tartan trolley, I've got a tartan trolley.

We'd both keep it moving, and never mention it when we'd see each other at school. But even worse than those times was being seen by a group of the 'cool' kids from school, on their way to go swimming or to spend their pocket money at JD Sports or Woolworths. *They* didn't have to go to the market with their mums.

The only thing I liked about going to the market was leaving the market, because that's when Mum would turn to me, hold out her hand and say, 'Here you are, here's a pound – you can buy yourself something.'

Rah! A pound!

Then I was faced with a choice. Do I go to the stall of warm doughnuts that I'd been smelling all day? Or do I go to the pound shop?

Who am I kidding? It was *always* the pound shop.

For us working-class kids, going to the pound shop was like going to Argos, except everything cost a pound. You could buy anything in the pound shop. A pillow, a toy gun that shot out bubbles, even a Swiss army knife. All for a pound!

Believe it or not, the best thing you could get from the pound shop was a poster. There were always posters of Bob Marley, or just a random ganja leaf. I got a *South Park* one and an Arsenal poster in there.

A few years later I went to HMV and realised that all the things in the pound shop were unofficial knock-offs. Clearly some guy with access to posters and a laminating machine was ripping us all off with his 10p prints. But I didn't care. I had a room that looked like something out of *Friday* or *The Fresh Prince of Bel-Air*.

The toys were all knock-offs as well. They were just cheap remixes of name brands. They didn't have Lego at the pound shop – they had something called 'Cube Blocks'. Instead of Scalextric, you had 'Electric Cars'. They even had a fake Action Man called 'Action Guy'. I would buy them, but they'd never last. They weren't great but hats off to the pound shop for allowing me to get the toys that I wanted but couldn't afford at the time.

I'd always hope we'd get a taxi home from the market – that was the dream, sitting in the back, listening to the dispatcher send minicabs all over south London. But we hardly ever did. The bus was only 30p for a child and 70p for an adult, so I could see why Mum would always make us take it.

We'd see it at the stop, about to pull away, and Mum would tell me to run ahead of her so we could catch it.

Mum! I'm pushing this tartan trolley and carrying this big blue bag of meat – and now you want me to run for a bus??

We'd get back to the estate and all my friends would be playing out. They'd see me coming, and they'd all shout over:

'Mo! Mo! Are you coming out?'

'Can I play out, Mum?' I'd ask.

She would never say yes right away. It was always, 'Maybe – when you have helped me at home.'

I'd have to help her unpack the food and put it all away. 'OK, *now* can I go out, Mum?' But she'd always be finding more things for me to do, like taking out the bins. She'd be scouting around for more jobs for me.

It used to piss me off! But I'd do it all. Anything for a chance to play out.

Some Saturdays, by the time I got out, I'd only have an hour or so before it was time to go back in. The White kids would say, 'I have to go home for my tea' and run off. *Tea.* That was what they called it.

The White kids ate the same tea every day, but it looked like fun: pizza and chips; pizza and beans. But not just any beans, beans with the little sausages in it! Those things were special treats for us. Nearly every night, we had chicken and rice, mutton and rice, rice and beans, or, if Mum was skint, corned beef and rice.

Some weekends, Adam would come over to my house, or I'd go over to his. Adam's home was my home, and my home was his. My mum would look after Adam, and Adam's mum would look after me.

When Adam came over, my mum would feed him the same meals we had every other night of the week. He'd be *lapping* up a plate of curried chicken and rice. 'This is lovely! What is it?' he'd say. Meanwhile for me it would be the third night that week I'd had that exact same meal. Whatever Mum cooked on a Sunday night, she made it last, freezing it in empty ice cream containers and pulling it out when she needed to give us an easy dinner.

Don't get me wrong, Mum's food was delicious. But as kids we never got a choice in what we ate. Takeaways were a rare and special treat; I guess that's what our cooking was to Adam – something different. But in our household, it was just the most cost-effective way to feed three kids.

In reality, we weren't poor. But we weren't rich either. The beautiful thing about my mum is that she always put us first. She always made sure we had food in the cupboard and a roof over our heads. But I knew back then there was a real shame in being poor, at least among us kids. You'd never admit it.

I'd say in school that my mum shopped in Sainsbury's but, really, we were shopping in Kwik Save. Or Somerfield. Or Netto, in Peckham. Ah, man, Netto in Peckham! It was a bit like a Lidl really: cheap and cheerful. The good thing about it was it had no security, so you could open packs of sweets and eat them. All the shoppers would be walking around Netto eating all the food.

It was more fun to go to Adam's house at the weekends. We only had a maisonette but Adam had a *house*, with a *garden*, which was cool. His mum used to work on weekends, so often we would be there with just his dad.

Adam's dad was so chilled! A proper geezer! He'd sit there watching the football results coming in on Teletext every Saturday afternoon, a packet of peanuts in one hand and an ice-cold beer in the other.

At Adam's we could do whatever we wanted. We'd be tearing around the house, or jumping up and down on Adam's mum and dad's bed. Or we'd take his dog for a walk in the woods nearby. We'd go off and have an adventure, build dens to hang out in, and come back and play *Crash Bandicoot* late into the night. Nothing was against the rules, so long as we didn't disrupt the football results. I used to *love* going round to Adam's house.

Going to Adam's was great but when I was at primary school, I went to a few other kids' houses to play and that was a real eye-opener for me. At the primary school I went to there were three types of kids. You had kids from working-class backgrounds, kids from middle-class backgrounds, and you had some kids that were just downright posh.

My classmates lived in a mixture of areas: Peckham, East Dulwich, Brixton. Some of them lived in big townhouses over in Camberwell. There's one road there called Grove Vale Road, which was made up of huge Edwardian townhouses. Nowadays, the majority of them have been turned into flats.

One of my friends, called Benjamin, lived on that road. I remember one time I went round to his, and his mum said she could drop me back at home after.

My head was in a whirl. *They've got a car? As well?! Woah!*

Benjamin had one *big* house. He had *all* the toys. Just loads of fun shit that he didn't even play with. His place looked like a miniature Hamleys. He had the genuine Batman toys and the *real* Action Man. I *loved* Action Man. Secretly, I wanted to slyly nick a couple of toys from Benjamin's. But I knew I never could or Mum would buss my arse.

I didn't know that I didn't have much as a kid till I started going to middle-class kids' houses and kept on seeing Action Man. They'd have big Lego constructions as well. No cheap Cube Blocks from the pound shop for these guys! When she could afford it, my mum would buy me little bits of proper Lego, like a fire engine, but these kids had the fire station!

'Whoa! You've got the fire station!' I'd gasp. 'The whole fire station!'

And these kids didn't even play with their toys. I'd be at their house playing with them, all excited, and they'd say:

'No, come outside, Mo! Come on!'

'I ain't going outside. Are you mad? You've got Scalextric!' I would only ever see these toys in the Littlewoods catalogue.

And my friend would be like, 'Yeah, I play with it now and then. But come out! Let's play with worms.'

'Worms?! I don't wanna play with worms! You've got a Super Nintendo! I wanna play *Mortal Kombat*!'

When we'd play out, Benjamin's mum would ask me to stay for dinner. Or *supper*, as they called it.

'Mosiah, would you like some supper? Would you like to stay?'

I felt like I was at Richie Rich's house and half expected them to have a butler or a roller coaster tucked away somewhere. I'd tell Benjamin, 'Your house is the best house!'

Before I knew it, it would be time to go home. Except that I didn't *want* to go home. I was fascinated by other kids' houses. When I'd get back, I'd push my bedroom furniture around my room – my bedframe was on wheels – into whatever configuration theirs was in, trying to get that middle-class feng shui.

My mum would ask me, 'How was it? Was it fun?'

'Yeah, it was *so* fun!' I'd tell her. 'We did this, then we did that ...'

Then Mum would go quiet sometimes, like she thought I'd had *too much fun*, and then she'd say that I couldn't go back. I always felt like my mum never really liked these posh parents. I never knew why.

Sometimes I'd catch her making comments under her breath, like 'middle-class yuppies'. On reflection I can see how it must have been hard for her to hear me going on and on about the toys these other kids had that she would never be able to buy me. As a kid, when your mum says no, you feel like you're being oppressed. You feel like your mum is saying no out of spite.

Now, I realise how insensitive it was for me to go on about what a great time I had at my rich friends' houses. I hope I never hurt her feelings. Because over time, I realised that the shiny, materialistic things weren't what made you happy in life.

People like Benjamin could go on holiday every single year. People like Benjamin's family could own their own house. But the sad reality was they didn't have a close community. They didn't have anyone they could borrow a cup of sugar from, or someone who could watch their kids if they had to go out to the shops. They didn't have people like Adam across the road, whose house was your house, where you knew you would always be safe. Benjamin had a lot, but he didn't have those things. I always felt thankful and lucky that I did.

The one thing I really appreciated was being part of a community.

• • •

On the best days in the summer holidays, we'd be on the estate playing football till it was dark. Your mum would call you in to eat, then you might even be able to go out again. *Living the dream!*

Because I wasn't at school the next day, Mum might say, 'You can watch *EastEnders*, then after that it's bed.' The trick was to watch it then just sit quiet towards the end at 8.30. If I was lucky, Mum would get a phone call and forget I was there. It was wicked:

Woah! I'm still up at nine o'clock, watching The X-Files*! I'm absolutely shitting myself ... but I'm still up!*

Eventually, Mum would see me, or remember I was still there, after her phone call. She'd be like, 'Ahem! Excuse me – up to bed! Now!' But I felt like I'd won a little victory.

• • •

I wasn't a timid kid, but I was cautious of climbing stuff and getting into nonsense. Because I knew ultimately if you're climbing something and your mum's friend sees you, she's gonna tell your mum.

'I seen him climbing on the roofs the other day!'

And that would be you grounded.

But we were naughty and always getting into stuff. There used to be little brick buildings around our estate with big electric boxes in them: they were back-up generators, or something like that.

Kids being kids, forbidden areas like that with electricity or gas stuff really excited us. It was almost like those danger signs – WARNING! DANGER OF DEATH! – were nectar, and we were the bees. We broke into them more than once. Luckily, none of us got zapped to death.

One time, we noticed an abandoned car that had been parked outside Adam's house for ages. You can tell a car's been on your estate a long time when the wheels start going flat. We used to jump on that car. And then we started sitting in it. We called it 'our car'.

'Yeah, this is our car!' we'd say to each other.

Obviously, we couldn't drive it or anything, so we'd just sit in it. The horn worked, sometimes. We were so happy sitting in that car outside Adam's house ... and then, one day, it just disappeared. We felt like we'd been robbed.

'Huh? What happened to our car?'

We couldn't keep away from the garages next to our estate. The majority of them were securely locked up, but there were a couple of open ones that nobody used so we'd make them into our gang HQ. Our den. We'd get an old sofa from the tip and put it in there. We'd sit chatting in the dark, because there were no lights.

Then, one day, the council would come, clear out the garage and lock it up, so we'd have to find a new den. We started hanging out in the nearby woods. We were always fascinated when we found grisly stuff.

'You'll never guess what I just found,' one of us would say.

'Show me!' we'd shout. And we'd follow our friend through the forest, half hoping – and half dreading – we'd see a dead body, like the kids from *Boyz n the Hood*.

But it was always just another dead fox. We'd all stand around, poking it with a stick.

We never dared to go to the woods at night-time, but in the day, it was our territory, like we were the kids from *The Goonies* or *Stand by Me*.

One day, we went there and stumbled across … some porno magazines.

At that age – nine or ten – we didn't really know much about sex or pornography. The rudest thing I'd seen by that point was *Eurotrash* and a couple of blue films on Channel 5, but it was all pretty tame.

These porno magazines were something else, though. They weren't the classy type like *Playboy*. These were next level, with names like *Fiesta* and *Escort*. They were also slightly damp because they had been rained on (at least, I *hope* it was rain).

We were excited but also a bit nervous of them, as well. One of my mates picked one up and put it in his coat pocket. We all started winding him up:

'What, so you're gonna *take* that?'

'Nah!'

'Ew, you're nasty!'

'No! I ain't taking it!' he said, calculatedly throwing it under a car.

We came back the next day to look for it. But, of course, it weren't there no more.

• • •

Mostly, my friends and I stuck around the estate, or the woods where we'd made our little paradise. But sometimes we went to Dog Kennel Hill where there was an adventure playground and a youth club. That was an important place for me throughout my childhood.

The playground was on an open piece of land in the middle of the city. It had everything a kid could need or want. On one side was the actual playground, with swings, ziplines and a football pitch for playing goalie-to-goalie. If it was raining, there was the indoor area where kids could paint, or learn to DJ, or do arts and crafts. At one point it even had a miniature farm, complete with goats. That's right, goats.

Amazingly, we used to feed them KitKats. I have no idea if KitKats are an appropriate diet for goats, but they wolfed them down.

At night, Frank, the guy who ran the adventure playground, would close the main gates and let the goats out of their pen. These big male billy goats with horns would swagger about everywhere. Nobody would dare to break in. I guess they were security goats.

Then, one day we went down and the goats had just gone. Was it health and safety? Foot-and-mouth? We didn't know, but we missed them being around, and feeding them KitKats.

There had always been this rivalry between my primary school and the others nearby, which made absolutely no sense. What were we really beefing about? *My sprinkle cake is better than your sprinkle cake? We have a better percussion class?*

But in the adventure playground we'd all be mates, mixed in together.

I wasn't the only one from my family who went. My older sisters would be there too. They'd be chilling with their friends and, of course, they'd never want to be seen with me: 'Mo! Don't hang around with me! Go and play on the swings or something!'

I remember one hot summer's day, I saw one of the boys hanging out with my sister wearing a pair of trainers I'd never seen in my life. As a kid, the shoes that your mum would get you would be from the market. High-Tech, Ascot, and Adidas 4-stripes (a.k.a the fake ones). Or, if you were lucky, you might have the odd pair of Reebok Classics. But the shoes I saw on this kid literally blew my mind. They were grey, with bits of neon green. And where the sole was meant to be there was just a big air bubble.

I looked around and saw this guy's friends were all wearing different versions of the same thing – white with neon orange, sky blue with bits of yellow – all with the same bubble on the bottom. These kids were literally walking on air.

I found out later those shoes were Nike Air Max 95s, but everyone called them '110s' because they cost £110, which was a huge amount of money to us back then (even though that type of high-end trainer would cost you £500 or more today).

Seeing the older kids that I looked up to wearing those trainers at the playground gave me something to aspire to. They were the original influencers. I knew I'd do whatever it took to earn myself a pair one day.

The adventure playground was a safe space, growing up. You would be looked after without being *babied*. And you felt like you were part of a community. No: you *knew* you were part of a community.

Like me, some of the kids had been coming there from the time they were infants through to their teenage years. It was within the heart of the community, allowing them to grow as kids, and keeping them out of trouble at a time when teens were left to their own devices. Loads of the kids actually ended up working there or discovered that they wanted to go into coaching or teaching.

Over the years, it became more than a playground. It was a safe space that gave the kind of support kids didn't get from school, like help with writing their CVs and landing their first jobs.

Dog Kennel Hill Adventure Playground holds a massive place in my heart, and, despite the threat of budget cuts, it still plays a part in the community today, allowing kids to have a safe space. It gives city kids everything from swing sets to play on and camping trips out into the countryside. I remember going on a trip to Wales with the youth club, mountain biking, abseiling and just hanging round a campfire, getting to meet kids from all over the UK. It was the closest us council-estate kids ever got to Center Parcs.

I'm not sure if kids still have safe places like that today. I hope they do ...

●   ●   ●

Everybody on the estates knew each other, and a big part of that was that we all went to the same local schools. Our days at primary school always started with assembly.

Ouch! I wince even thinking about it now! We all had to sit cross-legged on the floor: our bony little arses on those hard wooden floors! When we reached Year 6 and finally graduated to sitting on the benches at the back of the hall, we felt like kings looking down on the peasants in Year 4 and Year 5.

Looking back, those primary school assemblies were fucked up. We were a real multi-cultural school, with kids from all kinds of backgrounds, but we only sang Christian hymns (then again, I didn't even *know* they were Christian hymns till I started going to weddings and recognised the songs in church).

I hated assemblies. We had folders with all the hymns in, and we'd be so bored that we'd all be sitting there, bending our folders into mad shapes. The teachers would spot us, and shout out:

'You! What are you doing there!?'

The only good assembly day was on a Friday, when the musical performances took place and everyone in the school was given a chance to get up on the stage and play music or dance.

I loved music class at my school because, for kids like me, it was a chance to express our creativity, without the pressure of getting a good grade. Except for most of us, we never got to choose the instrument we knew we were good at.

When it came to choosing our instruments, it always seemed to be the middle-class kids who got to pick first. This did my head in because I *really* wanted to play the drums.

No chance!

They would give me a woodblock! I remember being given two woodblocks and told to make a sliding sound. I found some rhythm and made it quite jazzy. The teacher was horrified:

'No, no, no, Mosiah! Just keep it simple, please!'

Other times, I would get given the metal triangle to ting. That was proper boring! The real bottom of the musical ladder.

In music lessons, you wanted to get on the big wooden xylophone. That was pretty cool. And the thing that was even better than that was the djembe drums.

If you could play the djembe drums in my school, you were a rock star, because not everybody could do it. The Black kids would be playing them well, then some White teacher with no rhythm would come over and try to show us how to do it.

The djembe drums were on a different level. Me and my friends would play them the only way we knew how. They're meant to be played with a strong rhythm but you don't really think hard about that, if at all.

We'd play the djembe drums in the traditional way, with them between our legs, and hitting a strong, natural rhythm. And the teacher would weigh in again:

'No, no, no, no! Not like that, please! That's far too aggressive!'

We used the bins in the playground as drums instead. It may sound mindless, but it wasn't; we were vibing and it was proper sick and creative. Best of all was playing djembe drums at the adventure playground, because they would let us go wild on them.

I just remember that it was so much fun, and if I can make a serious point, giving kids that outlet to be creative is so important. My creativity was nurtured from a really young age. I can see all of the ways that it's impacted my life, and I'm sure it's part of the reason why I'm doing what I'm doing today.

• • •

I was a pretty happy kid at primary school. We weren't wealthy, but Mum always made sure I was smart and well turned out. And as I got older, of course, clothes – specifically brand labels – started getting more important to me, to the point when I started nicking my sister's cool trainers and wearing them to school.

My friends were impressed ... but my mum was less so. She worked at my school and spotted me walking the corridors.

'Mo! What you doing with them on your feet?' she asked me. 'If your sister finds out, you're in big trouble!' And just like that the jig was up. After school, I had to dash home, clean up the trainers and put them back in my sister's room before she noticed.

But I couldn't shake the feeling that came with the attention and popularity kids gave me when I wore cool shoes, and it sparked what would become my lifelong obsession with trainers.

•   •   •

When we finished Year 6 at primary school and were all leaving, we had a farewell party and did an end-of-year school show. The whole class did a synchronised dance to Jennifer Lopez's 'If You Had My Love'. Actually, it was a pretty cool performance, if I say so myself.

And then, we were all crying. All of us kids, crying and saying things like 'I can't believe we're gonna leave here!'

It was emotional. We had all grown up and been together since nursery. We had been hanging out since we were babies. We were all bawling and signing each other's T-shirts.

'Sign my T-shirt, please! Say something on my T-shirt!'

It was sad, but exciting at the same time. For the first time in our lives, we were no longer protected by the invisible bubble we'd grown up in – where everyone knew everyone, where you could play out with your friends all day every day, and where you knew that if you fell over and scraped your knee, someone would give you a plaster and it'd all be OK.

•   •   •

Those primary school years are so special. You grow up, mature and leave them behind, but at the time they're so intense and your little world means everything to you. I will never forget how they felt, and how exciting everyday life seemed to be. Even though nothing much really happened.

By the time we left Year 6, we felt like kings. We'd only been here for a decade and a bit, but in our small bubble we felt like we knew it all. Little did we know, life was only just beginning.

2

THAT MOMENT WHEN ...

You Don't Know Who's Family and Who's Not

We couldn't spend the entire six weeks of the summer holiday playing out. Sometimes, you had to go away. And where you went depended on where your relatives or close friends lived.

If your parents couldn't afford to take time off work, you were likely to spend some of your summer holidays with relatives. Childcare was expensive, so it made sense for kids to go and spend a couple of weeks with their cousins or grandparents.

Then again, for most Black families, 'cousins' is a very loose term. Going to your cousins' can simply mean staying at your mum's best mate's house so that she can look after you along with her own kids. Recently, since becoming successful, I've found a lot more 'cousins' coming out of the woodwork …

Of course, you'd rather stay at some places than others. There was the favourite cousin you always hoped you'd get to stay with, the one with all the cool toys you didn't have and the mum who let you stay up all night watching TV. But as a kid you didn't have a lot of say in the matter. Sometimes you didn't even know you were staying with someone till you realised your mum had already left.

• • •

I spent a lot of summer holidays in Wales. My mum comes from there and I've got loads of family in and around the Cardiff area, so every few years I'd get packed off to stay with aunties and uncles. We never went on big holidays; visiting family was the closest we got. It's why my extended family is still so close: because we always made the effort to visit each other.

When Mum, my sisters and I would arrive in Cardiff, someone from my family would meet us at the train station and take us back to a house full of other relatives, who'd all spend the first twenty minutes crowding around me and telling me how much I had grown:

'Aww, Mo, but you're so big now!'

As a kid I was really shy and would often hide behind my mum, but a few hours and two Panda Pops later and I'd be on the dancefloor showing off my best Michael Jackson impersonation.

There were so many of them, and I wouldn't always know which ones were my real relatives at all. It led to confusion. Every person my mum was introducing me to, I automatically thought was a member of my family. Then later I'd find out that the kid I thought was my cousin wasn't actually family at all: our mums were just friends.

You know what, though? It didn't matter, because when you are a kid you just want to play, and if you get on with your 'cousin' they do feel like family ... especially if you see them every summer.

When I went to Cardiff and was playing out with my cousins and their friends, the other kids would be fascinated by me. I was different – the Black kid from London who showed up in his sister's cool trainers – and, I guess, seemed exciting. They were curious about who I was. And weirdly enough the girls fancied me. (See what a pair of Nike Airs can do, guys?)

I'd be grinning while thinking, *I'm not here for a long time, but a good time!*

I made some good friends on those trips. One year I met this boy the same age as me and I spent two weeks jamming with him, pretending we were Mike and Marcus from *Bad Boys*. We'd do everything from climbing trees, to searching for coral on the beach in Jackson's Bay, to burying each other in the sand, but at the end of those weeks when our holidays ended, it was 'Take care, see you later!'

And I never saw him again. That's just how it worked back in those days.

•   •   •

Apart from Wales, I'd never really left my estate, except for the odd school trip. When you grow up in a working-class environment, it's rare you get to travel to different parts of the country. I only got to see the wider parts of the UK once I started gigging.

How are you supposed to get around? Most low-income families don't have a car, and trains are expensive! That leaves the coach, and who's going to take the coach to the Scottish Highlands? Most Black communities are still in major port cities like Cardiff, Bristol, Liverpool and London, because that's where they first arrived and where their families settled, and so those are the types of places I got to see.

My granddad lived in a huge townhouse in a part of Cardiff called Grangetown that had a big West Indian, Asian and Somali community. It made me feel as if I was in London ... till they started talking in Welsh accents! *That* always threw me.

My granddad was a short, stocky Jamaican man who loved cricket. When we turned up at his house to visit, we'd be left outside for ages, even though we'd rung him up an hour before to let him know we'd be coming.

We'd be standing there, patiently pushing and pushing the doorbell, but Granddad wouldn't hear us for the longest time.

When he finally stirred and let us in, we'd walk into Granddad's house. It had red floral carpet (old person's carpet), which was kept fresh by a weird plastic runner in the hallway. To its left was the formal sitting room.

That room got used maybe once a year, usually on Granddad's birthday. It was *pristine*. It had pictures of all his grandkids, his old hi-fi, his fine china set and his drinks cabinet with all his rums. But *nobody* was allowed to sit in there. Not even visitors. All you could do was peek in as you walked past.

I still picture Granddad's house like it was yesterday. He had a long spare room with a big chest freezer in (ethnic minority families love a chest freezer). That was hardly used, either.

In his main front room, he had his grandfather clock on the wall – *TICK! TOCK! TICK! TOCK!* – above the fireplace and a huge plasma TV in the corner, like a little cinema screen. He'd always be watching cricket with surround sound, super loud.

I could see why the doorbell stood no chance! His TV was so big, it was like he had his own front-row seat at Lord's.

There was a protocol – an etiquette – to visiting Granddad. You had to dress smart and make sure your shoes were polished, scrub any dirt from your fingernails, even make sure you had no earwax.

You knew you'd always get offered a fizzy drink, usually a sugar-free Lilt because he was diabetic. It might sound weird now but, back then, this was a real treat. My sisters and me would be all excited:

'Yes please, Granddad!'

I remember opening his big double-door fridge once and finding it stocked full of multi-packs of these cans. I'd be so gassed sipping on my fizzy drink (in more ways than one).

In fact, you know that thing where you only slightly open the can, and suck out the drink through the crack, to make it last? I did that all the time as a kid! My mum would be staring at me and I would see the thought bubble over her head:

You better open that can proper or I'm gonna buss your arse about you sucking drinks! Are you mad?

My sisters and I would sit drinking our fizzy drinks, and being bare quiet and humble, waiting for Granddad to ask the question about how we were getting on in school. He'd ask each of us each in turn.

'How are you getting on in school?'

'OK, Granddad!'

'Good, Granddad!'

Then he would ask us if we had been helping out around the house.

'Yes, Granddad!' I'd say. And my mum would stare at me, that big thought bubble over her head again:

These lying little shits!

But the crucial bit about going to Granddad's was that he'd always give us a little bit of money. That was what you were really waiting for. In fact, let's cut to the chase here, that was the appeal when you went to *any* of your older relatives' houses. They would give you money.

Man, if Granddad gave us £20, I felt rich! I felt like I could buy a house. That was a serious amount of money when you were eight years old!

I also knew that if Granddad gave me money, I could use it towards something else. My mum couldn't normally afford to buy me big stuff outside of Christmas. However, if I wanted something badly and I got most of the money from elsewhere, then I knew that she might chip in with the rest, if it wasn't too much.

So, there was always a lot riding on this visit to Granddad!

Sometimes, it would go down to the wire. We would be sitting there for two hours and the visit would be getting all wrapped up. Mum would be saying goodbyes and getting ready to stand up and there was still no sign of any cash coming out.

I'd be looking hard at Granddad, wondering: *Big man, where's the money? Where's the cash?*

I must have looked like that staring Diddy meme! Then Granddad would stand up and say, 'Hold on a sec, let me go upstairs and get a likkle summin' for the kids … '

Hallelujah! But sometimes he'd completely forget and you'd get nothing, and it would have been a wasted journey. Well, except for the fizzy drink, I suppose.

I remember one time me and my sisters were staying with Granddad and not really enjoying it. We had a little secret meeting, plotting about how we wanted to go home because we were hating it there. It was OK there, I suppose, but we were missing home.

We didn't manage to escape, but we did wake up early the next morning so that we could watch Nickelodeon before Granddad put the cricket on. And, one time, we did the most audacious thing ever. We went into his best sitting room (the room nobody went into), opened a drawer, and found a box of hazelnut chocolates.

We all took a chocolate. One each. At eight years old, it felt to me like the crime of the century! *Mission Impossible*!

That visit was the first time we couldn't wait to get back home. We were so excited to see my mum at Paddington. I was crying because I was so happy.

We didn't just go to my Granddad's. Sometimes we'd go to stay with Uncle Steven, my mum's brother, I used to love going to his house because I knew he used to have remote-control planes. *Wow!*

Uncle Steven used to promise that we would go to the fields behind his house and fly them. He said that every year. We never flew those planes, not even once. Come to think of it, I'm not sure I ever even saw them …

Despite his remote-control planes never leaving the runway, I liked staying with Uncle Steven because he was funny. I have always said that I get my comedy and sense of humour from my mum's side of the family, and I think Uncle Steven proves it.

The weird thing is, I can't really explain how funny Uncle Steven is. Like, his jokes wouldn't even look funny written down here. It was all in his delivery. His charisma, his charm and his wit made him hilarious.

Uncle Steven looked like your typical dad. He had a thick moustache and was covered in tattoos from his time in the army. One time, he came to my mum's fiftieth birthday party at a pub in Forest Hill. Another uncle, Uncle Terrence, arrived in a super-long leather jacket, thinking he looked like the *bee's knees*, and Uncle Steven asked him, 'Where you fuckin' goin'? The fuckin' *Matrix*?'

Burn! Uncle Terrence must have spent a lot of money on that coat and his face showed he knew that he might as well throw it in the bin right now. I was crying so hard. From that moment on, it would always be *The Matrix* coat.

You know, I was right – when I look at that joke on the page, it doesn't look all that funny! I guess you had to be there. But believe me, Uncle Steven was a funny man.

I've got a lot of other uncles on my Granddad's side in Wales – Zach, Kelvin, Mike, Joseph – and they're all cool. They always had nice cars and houses and they were always going abroad on holidays. Growing up, I aspired to be like them.

When I was about eight years old, Uncle Zach got married. I still remember how cool that day was. Mum got me a Ben Sherman suit and I thought I looked so slick in it. Uncle Zach had hired out a big golf course, and my cousin and me took the opportunity to work the door.

We started charging all the guests to come in. We took a pound from the guys and asked the women for a kiss on the cheek. We were only kids but we were moving like grown men! It was a real hustle. We made quite a bit of money that night.

Looking back, I enjoyed visiting the family. Today, I'm still close with my cousins, but it's not as easy to see them because everyone is busy and has their own families these days. But we always try to make the effort for big events.

Of course, the rules have all changed for me now. It's the next generation of my family, so if it's not me doing the long-distance driving, it's my relatives bringing their kids to see *me*. But instead of hoping that I'll give them some money, being twenty-first-century kids, what they want most is for me to follow them back on Instagram or join in on one of their TikTok videos.

3

THAT MOMENT WHEN ...

All You Care About at School Is Drama and Football

Ludo et Theatrum

When we left junior school, we all went off to different secondary schools. By default I got into the school in my local catchment area, but my mum didn't think it was very good back then and didn't want me to go.

A lot of us got into Pimlico Secondary School. So …

Boom! Here it is. Year 7!

I'll never forget my first day.

Pimlico School was quite a long way from where I lived but there was one bus which took us all the way there – the 185. When I got to the bus stop, there were about eight of us from my primary school.

'We all know each other, so they might as well put us in the same class,' we all said to each other. That was what we hoped would happen.

Well, when we got to secondary school, all the Year 7s had to go to a special assembly. It was like when you watch one of those prison films and the newbies are getting booked in. Everything felt strange, and different. And there was a major, important difference in this assembly. We weren't sitting on the floor no more. We now, finally, got to sit on proper chairs. It was all so new.

The teachers in the assembly started reading out our names for which classes we would be in – 7.1, 7.2, 7.3 and on – and one by one, all of my friends started being taken away into different classes.

Oh, man, there goes another one! I thought we were all gonna be in the same class together!

It was so stressful because I had wanted to be in a class with all my friends. Luckily, three of my friends – Louis, Simeon and Joshua – did get put in my class.

The school looked enormous to us. Some kids in Year 7 were taller than us, and we weren't used to that. We were thinking *This is big, bruv! Shit, man!* But nothing prepared us for the next day, when the older years came back to school.

There were kids in Year 11 who were so tall, they looked like adults. Some of them even had facial hair! Us Year 7s felt like little penguins sneaking past the walruses, hoping to slip by unnoticed.

The school was sort of liberal and we didn't have to wear uniforms. So, there were all these sixteen-year-old kids walking around dressed like proper teenagers.

I remember one Year-11 kid was bouncing his basketball on the concourse. A teacher came along and was like, 'Excuse me, can you stop doing that, please?'

And the pupil just said, 'Shut up, man!'

What?! I'm seeing people disobey teachers. I couldn't believe it.

It all felt surreal. There was so much to get used to. We met all our teachers, and one of them said he was the art teacher.

Huh? They have teachers here just for ART??

Those first few days in Year 7 opened my eyes to so much but, of course, the more time we'd spent in secondary school, all of that weird stuff began to feel normal. Well, as normal as anything can feel when you're an adolescent whose hormones are all over the shop.

Secondary school is such a peculiar time because nobody really knows what they want to do with their life. Well, maybe a few kids do, but I didn't have the first idea and nor did most of my mates. We were just getting through life day by day without any real idea where we were going or what we were doing.

For a few years, I wanted to be a professional footballer, and I didn't really care about lessons. At all. I was just fucking around and never really bothered with anything. I mean, I'd get my work done, but once that was out of the way, whether my answers were right or wrong, I'd be talking and being a bit of a class clown. I think, subconsciously, I had told myself *I don't really give a shit about none of this stuff*!

I couldn't be bothered with learning subjects like geography. I couldn't even find any interest in the more important ones like English and maths – and a lot of the reason was that I struggled to take an interest in things I knew I wouldn't use in real life. I thought there was no point in me doing it.

But it wasn't just my lack of interest that was to blame. Sometimes I found the work too hard, or just didn't get it, because I was dyslexic, and support was hard to come by. My school could only stretch its resources so much.

There's no way around saying this. As a dyslexic Black boy in school, you get pushed to one side. There is an underlying, subconscious belief among some teachers that, as a Black kid you're not very intelligent anyway. That is compounded by dyslexia – especially if it goes undiagnosed, as mine was.

I know a lot of dyslexic kids don't get tested for the condition till later in life, or, even if they are diagnosed, are too embarrassed to tell anyone when they need help.

So, my choices for which subjects I studied at Pimlico were pretty random. I remember I chose business studies, but there was no real thought behind that decision. In business studies class, we had to make keyrings and sell them on the school concourse for a fiver each.

Ker-ching!

I enjoyed making a bit of money like that, but that seemed like the only good thing about the course to me. Business studies is an important subject but I wasn't interested. Capital gains? What teenager cares about *capital gains*?

So, I just stopped going to the lessons.

I would turn up at science lessons, but that was pretty much all that I did. *I turned up.* I liked certain aspects of science. I liked it when the teacher talked about the solar system, or when we did biology. But when we had to learn the periodic table for exams ... I couldn't be arsed.

I'd think to myself, *Am I gonna need this information when I leave here?* The teachers said that I would, but I knew I wouldn't. I knew that I wasn't going to go for a job and get asked which element sits between aluminium and phosphorus on the periodic table (it's silicon, by the way – I know that because I just looked it up).

There are times when I look back on school and think I could have tried harder. But when I think of the lessons I really honed in on, that were important to me, I know that it's those that set me up for later on in life.

• • •

Because I had so little interest in school, my life was still centring around what I did outside of it. I was still spending a lot of weekends with Dad in Brixton – although Brixton back then was nothing like it is today. Nothing at all!

Brixton is well gentrified nowadays but back then it was a real melting pot of cultures. There were people from all walks of life and all ethnicities, mixed in together, going about their business and going to the churches, mosques and temples. There always seemed to be a sound system playing.

The market was so central to Brixton then. It was such a hub, always busy and bustling, everybody shouting and getting their meat and fish and veg. The fish looked so fresh, like it had just come out of the sea. Being a kid, hanging out at the market didn't really interest me, but as an adult I love the buzz and energy of it.

The most important place in Brixton for me was Jackets. It was a jacket potato takeaway that let you have absolutely anything you wanted with a jacket spud. It was well ahead of its time. I can't believe it hasn't made a comeback! Dad used to take me there all the time because I loved it so much.

Dad had got a mobile phone when they first came out in the 1990s and he'd give it me to call Mum to tell her I'd be home soon. I'd be outside Jackets, with one of those big, old-school mobile phones with an aerial, telling Mum what time I'd be back. I never got any hassle – I don't think cell-phone jacking had been invented then!

Dad would still get me stuff sometimes, especially for birthdays. I always had this thing, though, that I wanted to be given money and choose my own presents. It was something that had been in my head ever since I'd overheard a conversation a few years earlier.

On one of my birthdays, I'd heard a friend of my mum's say to her, 'You must always give him money for his birthday, because that helps him to grow as a child.' That idea stuck with me – *Yeah! I like the sound of that!*

So, every birthday, whenever people asked what I would like, I'd say, 'Money, please!' I'd open a card from my aunty: '*Rah*, £20! Oh, and thanks for the card!' And as I entered my teens, I struck gold dust.

On my thirteenth birthday, Dad gave me £500. £500! He'd never given me anything close to that much before. I guess he must have thought that becoming a teenager is a special occasion.

'Go shopping! Get whatever you want!' Dad said.

I. Went. Crazy!

Dad and I went straight down Brixton High Street. There was a little bit of the street that had everything I wanted: Foot Locker, with a JD Sports and a Woolworths opposite. We got there and I filled my boots.

Straight off, I bought a PlayStation 2 console. Hardly anybody had one in those days, so it was a real big deal. I bought two games to go with it. One of them was *Grand Theft Auto III*. You had to be eighteen to buy it, but the assistant just looked at me and said, 'You're with your dad, yeah? OK, sweet.'

I bought a few DVDs, including the first *Fast & Furious*, then went into the sports shops and bought sick clothes and trainers. Bruv, I got through well over £400 in no time at all! It was easy. I thought I'd died and gone to heaven.

'Let's get some food!' said my dad. We went to the Wimpy, we ordered our food, and then Dad said to me, 'You can pay!'

Huh? Spending my birthday money buying lunch for my dad – how did that work, exactly? But I knew my dad had just watched me spend £400 in an hour. I could hardly complain!

After we ate, we went to my dad's house. Some of his Rasta mates were there, so we set up the PlayStation, played a few games and then all watched *Fast & Furious*. And I sat there thinking, *This is the best day of my life!*

• • •

The other thing I explored when I was about thirteen was music. This meant being exposed to the most prominent sound in the UK at the time: garage. Later on, grime came and most kids at the youth clubs were experimenting with that, whether that was trying to MC or learn how to DJ.

I was exposed to garage because my sisters listened to it. But as I got older grime started to take over. It was the underground, up-and-coming music of the youth at that time, like drill is today. Sidewinder was a huge grime event that showcased some of the UK's biggest underground MCs – Wiley, Dizzee Rascal, Heartless Crew – and the recordings of those shows were legendary. You'd have a double cassette tape of these shows – the most famous one was of Dizzee Rascal and DJ Slimzee. But almost nobody had the original. You'd get the pound shop TDK 90 cassette tapes from your friend, who'd got them from their friend, and so on, and then you'd have to copy them and hand them back. And you had to do it quick because it was the one thing everyone would demand to get back. Those tapes were precious!

It was so different to music today, where everything is documented. Back then, you didn't even know what half these MCs looked like. You'd hear them on the radio, and if you missed a set, you missed it. Recordings were rare till MySpace came along, and eventually Roony Keefe's cult DVD series *Risky Roadz*, which documented the early days of grime for fans at a time when YouTube and Instagram didn't exist yet.

You'd also hear grime at youth clubs, and most of them, at least the ones in London, had decks.

They would have a little sound system, and there'd always be that one kid who knew how to DJ. Back then, vinyls were cheap at £5–10 apiece, but having full home set-up was rare.

There was always a DJ somewhere in your area. And everyone used to MC, or *try* to MC, in front of the bedroom mirror or out on the playground. If you happened to be friends with someone who was a DJ, that was even better because you were both helping each other.

That was how a lot of crews started out. A lot of So Solid Crew came from the same estate in Battersea. That allowed them to all lean on each other at a time when they didn't have many resources like that. Back then, it was all about power in numbers. The bigger your crew, the more people knew who you were.

I remember a time being at the youth club in Dog Kennel Hill and everyone going back to back. Some people were actually really good at spittin'. Everyone was going up on the mic and, naturally, I wanted to get involved.

Having your staple sixteen bars meant a lot, and every time it was your turn to spit, you did your best to sound good. The guys who took it seriously would walk around with a notepad full of lyrics. Others, like myself, would just try to rhyme and hope we wouldn't fumble our words.

The craziest thing with grime is the tempo. It's 140bpm (beats per minute). Hip-hop is 75bpm, maybe 80bpm. I'm not an MC but I can spit (in fact, that's pretty much how my geezer character came about years later, when I was just spittin' for fun).

If it wasn't for youth clubs, I don't think grime would have existed in the same way. That's where a lot of stuff was being recorded and produced. Professional recording studios weren't that expensive but, even if you had the cash, you weren't spending it on an hour's studio session.

I remember one time we were spittin' in the youth club and the mic came to me. I started spittin' some nonsense. The buzz was ferocious but I didn't know what I was talking about. I was talking real crud.

'*I'll come to your mum's house and I'll pull out her eyeballs,*' I said. *Shit!* I was thirteen, and I definitely wasn't pulling out anyone's mum's eyeballs! That's next level. But you wanted to sound dangerous because the whole point of MC'ing was to be dramatic.

The words sounded violent but they were part of the stupidity of the whole thing. It wasn't meant to be real or taken literally. *You don't wanna bring arms out / I'll bring arms out to your mum's house!* No one was actually about that life. We were just kids – we weren't even shaving yet!

The big thing you hoped for when you were spittin' on the mic was to get a 'wheel up' (a rewind). That's when an MC was so good, everyone would lose their shit and the DJ would have to pull up the record and rewind the track. They weren't easy and, no matter how hard I tried, I never once got a wheel up. But I liked it when people would clash each other on the mic.

So, yeah. I would go and try to spit some bars about pulling someone's mum's eyes out. And then I'd go home and do my Key Stage 3 homework, which all felt entirely natural.

To this day, I've still never got a wheel up.

• • •

Like any kid, I'd hang out with my mates in the evenings and at weekends. Sometimes we would go swimming at Brockwell Park's outdoor lido. It's weird that our parents let us just go like that: I bet kids don't have that kind of freedom today. I think our parents just figured, *Oh, they're all together – they'll be OK! They can look after each other!*

I could swim OK, but I had this fear of the deep end of the pool. The other boys were jumping right in there but I hated it when I couldn't feel my feet on the bottom of the pool. So I developed a mad cover story.

Instead of going in the pool – I lay sunbathing.

I came home from Brockwell Park and my mum said, 'Woah, you have gone *black*!' And it was all because I didn't want to jump in the deep end.

Other times we would go swimming at Camberwell Leisure Centre. We'd swim for two hours then walk down to McDonald's for a Big Mac, and maybe hang out and try to chat up some girls in Ruskin Park. Because, like any hormone-laden adolescent, I was beginning to get *very* curious about activities that wouldn't qualify for a PG-13 rating …

•   •   •

Thinking right back, my first awareness of sex probably came at the end of my time at primary school, when I first watched *Eurotrash* on TV. I was like, *Woah! What is this, bro? A vagina with a bush? Oh my gosh!* I didn't really get a lot of what it was all about … but I knew that I wanted to know more.

But even after finding the porno mags in the woods as a kid, and seeing *Eurotrash*, I still didn't really know much about sex till one night when I was about thirteen. I was going over to see a friend, Rashid, and I asked my mum if I could sleep over at his house. Mum was cool with that and she said yes.

But I didn't stay at Rashid's house. We went over to see a friend called Ishmael, who was a little bit older than us. Ishmael lived on a big estate in central London, and our night there was proper strange.

Ishmael was one of those kids who looked and behaved a lot older than he was and seemed kind of worldly, like he knew more than the rest of us. He was just more clued up about everything … and that included porn.

Ishmael's family was out, so we were on our own in his front room. Before I knew what was happening, he'd put a real porn film on the VCR for us to watch. Bear in mind, at this age the whole concept of sex seemed crazy to me. I didn't really know what was what, or what it was all about.

I'd sometimes hear older kids at school saying that someone had 'slept with' somebody else and I literally thought that that was all it meant: that they had slept in a bed together. *Maybe they had kissed and cuddled a bit?* So, what I saw at Ishmael's house properly blew my mind.

What. Is. This?

What am I watching here?

Is that what people really do?

What … THAT goes in THERE?

I didn't say anything at the time but, if I'm honest, I was slightly disgusted at what I was seeing. But at the same time, I was curious …

After I had seen the porno at Ishmael's house, I discovered the adult channels on Sky. If you timed it right, these channels would do a ten-minute preview of the pay shows.

At the end a voice would say, 'If you want to see some sexy stuff, make sure you call this number!' and a phone number would flash up on screen. I used to think, *One day, when I'm old enough, man, I'm gonna call that number!'* That was my dream!

I used to try to guess the password to watch the adult stuff but could never crack it. Then one day, at school, a kid said to me, 'Don't you know? It's the last four digits of the number on your Sky card!' And he was right – I couldn't believe it!

Once I was in, that night, I watched all the adult channels, from TelevisionX to Playboy. But the funny thing was, you'd see people having sex, but you wouldn't – the screen was all fuzzy, and the way they filmed the scenes, you still couldn't really see anything! I was fuming.

• • •

As I grew up, I got fixated on getting a part-time job to earn some money so I could do stuff. Everyone wanted a moped back then, specifically a Gilera Runner or a Typhoon. You were one of the coolest guys on the block if you had a moped. I wanted one *real* bad.

One time, Mum told me about a job going at the market on Walworth Road. She said there was a fruit-stall holder who was looking for helpers.

I went down to the market, found the stall and introduced myself to the old White guy running it. He said I could start the next week, but I took one look at the place and knew I wouldn't be going back. Even at that age I knew I only wanted to do work that I would enjoy.

So, I never did save anywhere near enough to get that moped.

I never got involved in crime and bad-boy shit, but I knew that it was around us. There was one boy in my area who was well caught up in it. He was bad news and always up to madness. My mum used to warn me: 'Don't hang out with him, Mosiah! He's a thief!'

I remember once seeing that guy out and one of the older boys on my estate asked him, 'Yo, bro, can you get me a tax disc?' The thief vanished and then reappeared three minutes later with a fresh tax disc from someone's car.

Why?! Even at that age, I thought, *What's the point of that? It's not going to have the same registration number as your car!*

At the time I thought it was just totally stupid. But looking back, I realise the boy was actually troubled. He wasn't doing it to be cool. He was doing it to earn a bit of money. His family never had much.

It just goes to show that when you're growing up, you're a product of your environment. I was one of the lucky ones, with a family that was loving and supportive.

•   •   •

School had got a bit better for me around Year 9, when I started doing drama and performing arts. I loved the lessons from the start – and a lot of it was down to my teacher, Miss Simpson.

Miss Simpson was cool without trying to be cool. She was a teacher but primarily, she was a real person that kids could relate to. She wasn't all about discipline like some of the teachers were, and you could tell that she knew all about what real life was like outside of the school.

Some teachers just ordered the kids around all the time, and that was that. We'd have PE teachers who'd make the kids do the lessons no matter how they might be feeling or what they were going through.

At that age, loads of boys go through body issues that they keep to themselves, dealing with all of the awkward changes of puberty and adolescence. But if they forgot their sports kit one week, some of the PE teachers would have no sympathy at all.

'Go to Lost and Found!' they'd shout at them. 'Find some kit that fits you and then come and join us in the sports hall!' They wouldn't consider that the boy might be crippled with embarrassment and not want to run around in somebody else's lost clothes. And that's not an easy thing to explain when you're a boy and nobody understands why you don't want to join in and play football.

In swimming, there were teenage girls who were developing quickly who didn't want to have to be in a swimsuit in front of their male peers, but the teachers would ignore that. They'd be even less sympathetic if a boy – me, or one of my mates – didn't want to swim.

'Don't be stupid – get in the pool!' they'd command. They'd have no knowledge of, or interest in, what was going through a kid's head:

Bruv, I don't have a swimming cap! If I swim, my hair is gonna get fucked and my skin's gonna be dry the whole day. It's gonna mess up my canerow! My mum'll be angry when I get home and I'll be coming into school with my hair looking shit tomorrow …

We never said those things to them. Because there was no point. We knew that they wouldn't listen to a bunch of thirteen-year-olds.

Miss Simpson wasn't like that. She would talk to us about her life. She was in her late thirties, and from the ends, and had two mixed-race sons, so she had insight into what growing up as a young Black boy in south London was like. She would say things to me and I'd be thinking, *Man, she knows what's going on! She just gets it – she gets us!*

If a kid came to drama lesson and said, 'Miss, I don't feel good today, I don't feel like doing anything,' she would say, 'That's fine – just chill out, watch and don't be disruptive!' But we normally *did* all want to do it. Because the lessons were great.

She would tell us, 'OK, let's devise a play!' The first time she ever said it to us, in my first drama lesson when I was thirteen, I had no idea what she was talking about.

'Huh? Devise a play? What does that mean, Miss?'

'I mean, make up your own story and develop a narrative!'

Rah! Sick!

Most of the boys would devise stories that were based on bank robberies and wrestling. They made absolutely no sense at all.

'OK, I'll be The Rock and you be Stone Cold Steve Austin!' they'd say. 'And we'll rob a bank!'

We'd always do drama in a classroom on blue PE mats, so we could roll around on the floor, if we had to, without getting hurt. This would help some of my classmates' stupid storylines:

'OK, Mo, I'm gonna choke-slam you now, innit?'

'What? Why are you gonna choke-slam me?'

'Because you robbed the bank, bruv!'

I didn't want to do choke-slamming or play wrestlers robbing banks, though. I wanted to do proper stories and cool, funny characters. Even at that age, I was inspired by actors who did impressions and voices: Jim Carrey, Eddie Murphy, Robin Williams. I loved watching them.

We would make up fun little stories and I'd try to do accents for my characters. Or I might have my character talk to the rest of the class who were being the audience halfway through the play.

'Ah, Mo, that is called breaking the fourth wall!' Miss Simpson would say.

Is it? I hadn't known that, but I was excited to be told and keen to learn more and more. I felt like playing characters in drama class was giving me a kind of freedom.

Drama lessons were also my first experience in school of getting to be the centre of attention and making people laugh. I remember our class doing a little play for the whole school in the assembly. The kids were bussin' up, and afterwards they were all telling me that I was really good.

That wasn't something that I was used to being told. But I liked it very, very much.

It wasn't just the kids who were praising me for the drama. I had been in drama class for maybe a couple of months when, one week, Miss Simpson took me to one side.

'Mo, look, you're extremely talented,' she told me. 'I really think that you should pursue performing arts, because you are very, very good at it.'

Woah! No teacher had ever said anything like that to me before. And I suddenly felt a million times taller.

I loved those drama lessons and I learnt things there that I took into my later life and I still take with me today. I started devising little scripts for plays and then it suddenly hit me: *Rah! I'm writing sketches! I'm a writer!* Then, I'd start directing those sketches in class.

A penny was dropping, and it was an amazing moment. Because, till then, I'd always thought that a writer was a *special* person with a golden, magic pen. A director had magical talent and sat in a *special* chair. And then I realised:

Rah! I know I'm good at drama, because Miss Simpson says I'm good at drama! So, I'm going to crack on with it – I can do this!

Miss Simpson was the first teacher who ever gave me – and a lot of other kids, as well – that kind of inspiration and motivation. She was the first one who made me feel good about myself. I still keep in touch with her today. When I have big shows, I invite her along and give her tickets. She might come with one of her kids, who are all grown-up and have their own kids now. She's been a big part of my journey, almost like a second mum at times.

I still call her 'Miss Simpson', even though I'm an adult now and I know her name is Rory. If she ever pings me a text, I get back to her right away, even if I'm busy:

Oh my gosh! I must call Miss Simpson back!

It's funny – Ashley Walters went to our school. He was there before my time, but I knew him as Asher D from So Solid Crew. The first time I ever met him was around 2015, outside a hotel in Birmingham at three o'clock in the morning, after I'd done a comedy show. I walked past and clocked him. I felt really nervous to approach him because he was with a group of his mates, but I did anyway. And the conversation went like this:

ME: Asher D, right? Hey, what's up?

ASHER D: Er, hey, what's up?

ME: Hey, I went to your school.

ASHER D: *Awkward silence.*

ME: You know Miss Simpson, right?'

ASHER D: Er, yeah … she was my teacher. She's great …

And that was the end of that chat. In my life I've had some awkward conversations, but that was up there as one of them. Nowadays, I count Asher as a friend and always think it's funny that the first time I tried to talk to him was about Miss Simpson. But the point is, she was that influential to my life that I couldn't not talk about her with someone who'd known her as well.

She's about to retire now. I've been back to the school a few times to see her, or to give talks, but if I am honest – and I know this might sound cold – I don't think I'll go back anymore when she's gone. It's not that Pimlico isn't full of excellent, dedicated teachers. It's just that to me, that school is all about Miss Simpson.

4

THAT MOMENT WHEN ...
Life Is All About Going Out

When you turn eighteen it feels like the biggest thing in the world. It feels like *adulthood*! And *freedom*! But the main thing it means is that you can start going out. Not *playing* out, no – proper grown-up *going* out.

When I was a kid, there was a symbolism to turning eighteen and being able to wave your ID at barmen and club bouncers. It meant that they couldn't refuse to serve you or turn you away, even if you still looked too young.

Well, that was what it was *supposed* to mean, anyway.

Before I turned eighteen, the biggest challenge was getting in the club to start with. I never went to clubs before I was old enough, but I know some people used to borrow older friends' or siblings' IDs. The Connexions card was particularly useful because it was free and doormen accepted it as proof you were old enough to buy drinks, even though it didn't actually include your date of birth.

Connexions was originally a career service for young people but it also offered help on things like housing, education, drugs, finance – everyday life stuff. The card basically let you get discounts in certain places and it became an unofficial ID for people that didn't have provisional licences or passports.

Having a Connexions card was a big deal because it also meant you could go to the corner shop and buy a lottery ticket or a miniature bottle of rum … even if you were pulling out a Velcro-strap wallet, because you were still only sixteen years old!

• • •

The early raving days from when I started going out felt special. It was before the days of camera phones and people would take digital cameras out with them. And after the rave, you'd see people handing out promo CDs because Spotify didn't exist then either.

Because my friend Rashid was a year older than me, he'd already been going out for a while, and sometimes I would go out with him and his mates. Before we went, we would always do pre-drinks and listen to some music at his house.

Somebody would always bring Lambrini. We tried to drink as much as possible before going out – but just the light stuff, like Bacardi Breezers and Smirnoff Ice – and listen to music or watch clips on early YouTube, like Techno Viking or silly cat videos.

There would be about five of us, and five guys trying to get into a club felt like mission impossible. We'd wait to get to the front of the queue, then the bouncers would say we couldn't come in. It bugged us, because we were just after a good night out.

You usually needed girls with you in order to get in. So we'd literally just be walking around trying to find girls to go in the club with us. (Girls got in for nothing but boys had to pay £20! What the hell was that about?)

We'd spot a bunch of girls in the street and go up to them:

'You alright, girls? We're going raving, where you lot going? You want to come in with us?'

'No, no, no, we're fine, thanks!' they'd say, shaking their heads. 'We're alright.'

'We're not trying to move to you, I swear down,' I'd promise them. 'We just wanna get in the club and we need your help.'

There would usually be one girl that showed a bit of compassion and thought about helping us.

'Yeah, maybe we should …' she'd say, and straight away, all of her friends would be like, 'Becky! No!'

Now and then, though, you'd come across a couple of good sisters who would say, 'Yeah, yeah, cool, man, no worries! We'll help you.'

Big up to those girls, man!

Back then, for some reason, I always wanted to get to the club for as soon as it opened. God knows why! Everyone knows that prime time is from eleven o'clock till one o'clock in the morning. Probably, I just wanted to get my money's worth! I didn't even have the money to be buying drinks all those hours. But at eighteen I just wanted to get in the club and do the Soulja Boy 'Superman' dance.

Crazy.

The thing about clubbing back then is that it wasn't always that much fun because you didn't really have money for drinks. You'd try to firm it by drinking water with some ice all night and passing it off as vodka lemonade.

That was the level of broke we were at. We'd have enough for one drink or, if we were lucky, two. Sometimes, we'd get so bored of tap water that we'd ask for sparkling water and lime, to spice it up a little bit and not look quite so boring. *Not quite.*

I remember going to one club just off Oxford Street with two friends, Mark and Louis. They clearly saw us coming a mile off. It was only an hour before closing time, but when we asked the bouncers how much it was to get in, they still said £20.

It was a rip-off, but we were out and we didn't want a flat end to our evening without having even gotten into a club, so we said 'Fuck it!' and paid. When we got downstairs, the party was still in full swing at three o'clock. For us it felt like it was too late for us to join in, but at that age we were just happy to be in a club.

Mark bumped into another friend, who had a proper *drink* drink. *Wow!* It made us curious how he could afford it, so I asked Mark:

'How did he get that? Did he get a free drink?'

'Sort of,' said Mark. 'He nicked it from a table.'

'*What?*'

The guy overheard us. 'Yeah,' he nodded. 'I did. I'll nick you one as well.'

This guy waited till people went on the dancefloor and then he took their drinks. He called it 'minesweeping'. I'd never heard of it before and I couldn't believe my eyes. I would rather swallow my own spit than drink a random person's leftovers.

• • •

When you're eighteen and going out, it'd be a bonus if you met girls, but it was often awkward for everyone because at that age you didn't have any money to even buy them a drink, it was purely about getting their number.

My friend Liam was the good-looking one, so girls weren't really interested in the rest of us anyway. All they wanted to know was, 'Who's your friend?'

Nobody was ever direct. At eighteen, you're shy, and public rejection kills you, especially in clubs surrounded by elders. This was no longer the school disco.

In my early days of raving, we danced a lot. I remember going to a rave in London Bridge at a club called seOne. This particular event we went to was big within the Chinese community. When we were approaching the club, they had their kitted-up Honda Civic and Nissan Skyline sports cars parked outside. It looked like a scene from *The Fast and the Furious*!

This was around the time of movies like *Step Up* and *You Got Served*, so that kid you knew who always used to body-pop finally had his moment to shine. The DJ started playing a song from the *The Fast and the Furious: Tokyo Drift* soundtrack called 'Tokyo Drift' by Teriyaki Boyz (if you know, you know) and before I knew it, a circle formed on the dance floor around one Chinese guy, who was popping and locking.

I used to dance at the raves and I had rhythm back then as well (nowadays, I just hold a little skank and lean against the wall). I was dancing, and minding my own business as you do, when suddenly my friends pushed me into the circle next to the body-popper.

He spotted me, and thought I was trying to challenge him, like we were in a high school dance-off. He had the crowd in the palm of his hand with some of the moves he was doing. I'll be honest, I didn't want to clash with him but I couldn't just leave the circle because everybody was crowded around us, making loads of noise.

OK. I made a plan on the spot. I would put my hand in his face, as if I was pulling it off, then pretend to throw it to the floor. The guy was right in my face, so I shoved my hand out ...

Boom! I accidentally pushed it right into his mouth! When I looked up he was shocked, and his lip was bleeding. Everybody was going absolutely crazy because they thought I had punched him in the face! I scurried away back in the crowd with my friends.

By that time, I had developed a special clubbing dance move. It was always my big finale. And I picked it up from watching WWF wrestling.

Anybody who watched WWF (or WWE, depending on how old you are) back then will remember Scotty 2 Hotty's signature move, 'the worm'. When he had won a bout, Scotty would jerk and wriggle around the ring on the floor, like a worm.

I started doing the same in the clubs. I'd do my little version of the worm inside the circle. Nine times out of ten it went down great, except one time I body-slammed straight onto the hard wooden floor!

Ouch! I firmed it though, and took the applause at the end, but my poor legs were aching ...

• • •

Like everybody, I started off going to local house parties between the ages of sixteen and eighteen. Then after that we branched out to clubs in the West End. For us, the main clubs were Sound, Bar Rumba, Storm and the Rainforest Café.

Then someone introduced me to bars in East Central, in and around the Bank and St Paul's area. They had a much older and more sophisticated clientele than the West End clubs. The events that people put on were better and we had better nights out.

Once we started going to these events, I thought, *Right, this is a grown t'in*g! No more trainers, as we couldn't get in wearing them, we needed hard-sole shoes and smart shirts to get in the clubs. It's weird, because dancing in hard-sole shoes for a long time kills your feet.

My friend Liam worked at John Lewis and had started wearing nice shirts and ties, so we would follow his lead when it came to wearing smart clothes. The other alternative we sometimes followed was wearing Vans, bootcut jeans and a cardigan to the club. Yep, there was a stage in 2007 when guys started going to clubs wearing colourful cardigans.

Cardigans! We was in the rave wearing cardigans!

It was mad, but it was what everyone was wearing back then. Topman and Zara were iconic for cardigans, especially the ones with the big JLS collars. They were the main-man cardigan pushers.

Looking at some of the clothes we used to wear back then is funny. When macs were in, I bought a white mac from Topman for £50. I was a medium but I bought it in extra-large. I guess it was the masculine thing of not wanting to wear tight clothes. I used to buy *everything* in XL.

But the main thing for me was that everybody else was walking around in black macs and I wanted to be different. I never saw anyone else in a white mac.

That was me: *the guy in the white mac!*

Looking back now, I actually did look like a lab technician.

But let me tell you, I thought I had completed life. I thought I was The Man. Nobody could talk to me. I'd be in the club in my white mac, with a drink, snapping my fingers to T-Pain's 'Buy U a Drank' (*'Baby girl, what's your name?'*).

Fashion was strange then. Everything had to be colour-coordinated or super colourful. There was a lot of creativity going on, with people making their own T-shirts and custom creps.

In any case, some of the best nights out were in the raves where no one cared too much what they were wearing. They were the club nights when people had gone out for the love of the music rather than to stunt.

I used to *love* the music. It was the era of UK funky house, so we used to make up dances or learn the bait ones before we went out. Around 2007–10 was one of the best periods for UK funky house. It was also a time where MCs were jumping on funky house riddims and spittin', adding a new layer to it.

I still remember the big songs: Crazy Cousinz' 'Bongo Jam', KIG's 'Head, Shoulders, Kneez & Toez' and Boy Better Know's 'Too Many Man'. While our elders had had garage and jungle to dance to, we had UK funky house, grime, garage and even dubstep.

Once, me and my friends thought of making up our own dance and putting it on YouTube, hoping it would get a few thousand views and become the next 'Migraine Skank'. It would have been wicked. Sadly, we never quite got around to doing it …

When it came to getting home from the club, everyone was in the same boat. Nobody was driving, we couldn't afford black cabs and Uber didn't exist yet, so we'd all climb on the bendy bus. I'd get the 12 bus from Oxford Circus.

The 12 would take me all the way to Peckham, then I'd get off and walk home. It was sick, especially in the summertime when it was bright by four o'clock. As I walked through the park at five o'clock in the morning with my clothes still damp I'd be slightly embarrassed as I saw people out for an early morning jog. I was one of those ravers who danced non-stop, so I'd sweat a lot. I'd be walking home a wreck, and fully sweating for free, but it was worth it.

It really was worth it.

• • •

As you grow older, other interests take over in your life and you don't go clubbing as much. It's ironic: when you *can* finally afford to go out raving, no one can be arsed because everyone is shacked up.

I'm not totally retired from clubbing. I still do the odd sesh every now and then. But I don't make the same dumb decisions I did at eighteen – like downing a bottle of Jack Daniel's at Rashid's house to avoid buying drinks in the club!

Because, between you and me, that never ends well.

Today, if I invite friends to meet up at my house before we go out, I get everything prepped. *Drinks? Check. Music? Check*. But there's always someone who arrives for pre-drinks early, when you're still in your towel, sat on your bed.

Big man, why are you here early? That half an hour was for me to sit on my bed and decide if I actually wanted to go out till four o'clock.

When I go clubbing now, the big thing is drawing up the perfect pre-drinks playlist to get you in the mood for raving. The pre-drinks playlist is so important, but with great power comes great responsibility.

I don't like it when someone includes obscure Japanese wood chimes from 1970, or baile funk, or Styles P on their playlist. Come on! *No one wants to hear your friend's cousin's new rap song right before going out!*

No, those are the guys who play music just for themselves, and that's not for me. You need a good party playlist. It doesn't matter if no one knows the songs as long as they're good and they set the right vibe. That's all that matters.

How do you know when a playlist is good? A big clue is when you hear a couple of tracks you don't know, but they're a vibe, and you secretly start Shazaming in the back of the Uber to see what they are.

In fact, that taxi ride from the house is crucial. I *love* it when the playlist transfers from the house to the Uber. *Rah!* Mind you, you need a good Uber driver, not one who wants to play you his own tunes instead:

UBER DRIVER: Oh, you going out tonight, boss? You need the party tunes, right? You from Jamaica? Let me play you something …

We exchange an awkward look in the back.

ME: Bossman, can I use your Bluetooth?

UBER DRIVER: Ah, it's not working, my friend!

ME: Ah, OK. Have you got an aux cable instead then?

UBER DRIVER: That's not working either! Let me put on the radio for you.

And before you know it, you're listening to LBC on your way to the rave.

But my nights out have changed now. I might go to a restaurant with my girlfriend, have a nice meal and a few drinks, or I might go to a club with some friends, get a table, then maybe head off to the casino. That's what we do because *that's the age we are. That's where we're at in our lives.*

Back in the day, I wasn't like that. I just thought: *Rah, alcohol! Let's drink it all and get drunk!* But if I could talk to eighteen-year-old Mo now, I would tell him: there's nothing wrong with that.

It's a rite of passage. You need to go through it, and I wouldn't change any of the mad adventures and nights out I had when I was younger for the world. They were amazing – and I had to go through that stage of life's journey to get to where I am now.

5

THAT MOMENT WHEN ...

You Get Told Off for Thinking

MO
_____
Worker Ant

When I left college, I knew that I had to get some kind of work to earn some money. And that meant that I had to write myself a CV.

I had first heard about CVs when I was about fourteen. My big sister was leaving school and said, 'Yeah I've gotta get my CV done.' *A CV!* It sounded so complex and mysterious. I can still remember thinking, *Oh my gosh! I can't wait to have my first CV!*

They don't prepare you for CVs at school, though, or teach you how to do them. It's annoying. Why don't they teach us the useful stuff? They're banging on about something stupid, logarithms or whatever, and you're thinking:

Why can't you teach us how to make CVs, blud? We're fifteen! We're about to go out in the big wide world and you're teaching us bloody algebra! This ain't gonna help me get a job! (Unless I'm gonna be a rocket scientist or something like that.)

So, after college, I thought, *OK, I need to write my CV.* Not that I had anything to put on it. The only jobs I had done was cleaning the skirting boards, washing the dishes and going to the corner shop for my mum to get her bread, top up the electric meter and milk. And that was *always* unpaid work.

I didn't even know where to start with my CV, I didn't have any kind of template for what it should look like. I ended up going online and searching for 'CV'. The first thing that came up was that I should start with my name, number and email address.

That was a problem to start with. I couldn't use my normal email address: it was something like *gohardorgohome@hotmail. com*. Imagine getting a CV emailed to you from *shooterman85@ hotmail.com*. You wouldn't get far with that, though there are definitely people who've tried!

I had to get a more normal email but in those days you couldn't just set up a new account on your smartphone. You had to do it on a desktop with a platform like Hotmail, Yahoo or AOL. Now, I'm not gonna lie, I wanted one of those dope emails like *myname@info.com* (in fact, I still want one).

I put my home address on my first CV! I don't think anyone does that shit anymore. Then I started the CV with a brief bit about me, and it read something like this:

My name is Mo Gilligan and I'm a hardworking individual that likes working well in a team. I can handle working well under pressure and I'm also a bubbly, charismatic person that gets on with everyone.

You always have to say that – but really, who likes and even cares about 'working well in a team' when you're slogging it part-time at Topman? All you wanna do is get the discount, get paid and go home. You have to sell yourself on the CV but none of it is really true, you're just telling them what they want to hear.

Then there's the section about your academic qualifications. I remember once I even put my SAT results from primary school

I don't know why my mum used to dress me like a little Jamaican man!

The best thing about looking back at old childhood pictures is seeing the mad clothes you used to wear.

This is that innocent school picture everybody has of themselves, where butter wouldn't melt.

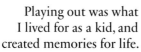

Playing out was what
I lived for as a kid, and
created memories for life.

With my friend Bob,
who lived down the
road. Basically one of the
reasons I support Arsenal.

Mosiah Gilligan
One of the funniest people in the
year! Always remember him
cracking joke by the pitch with
everyone because he's that
friendly. Star footballer, actor &
probably anything else he puts his
mind to. Miss him & everything

With Markus, Peter and Rashide, who I would go
out with in my late teens at Bar 101 (which is no
longer there).

Going out with Louis and Graham in our early
twenties, with me wearing my XL mac coat. At the
time I thought I looked really cool, but looking
back I actually looked like a lab technician!

At Dulwich Hamlet with Adam Wadmore after one of my early gigs in 2009.

Performing at a gig called The Lol Show at High Wycombe when I first started doing comedy.

At a university ACS show. I think I performed at almost every university ACS show in the country between 2009 and 2014.

This was my first business card, which felt like a really big deal to me, but I never actually ended up needing to give it out.

Mo The Comedian

Comedian - Host - Actor - Presenter

Facebook: Mo* The Comedian
Twitter: @MoTheComedian

MOTHECOMEDIAN.CO.UK

My Oyster card was my Uber back then – the only way I was able to get from gig to gig.

Myself with James Massiah, a poet I'd perform with at The Sunday Show. He became a great friend and has since gone on to do brilliant things in his career.

The Lol Show in 2013 at Bloomsbury Theatre, with Axel Blake, Travis Jay, Dane Baptiste, Aurie Styla, Babatúndé Aléshé and Mikey Carpenter. This was pretty much the generation of comedians that I started my comedy career alongside.

This was my first ever solo show, which I'd put on myself for my comedy night, Cracking up Comedy, in 2014.

Once I finished posing for this picture, we were told to take all these posters down.

Dave after-party in Edinburgh with some of the UTC gang: Emmanuel, Dane Baptiste, Kae Kurd, Kate Lucas, Tez Ilyas.

Me as the Geezer, the character that really took off online.

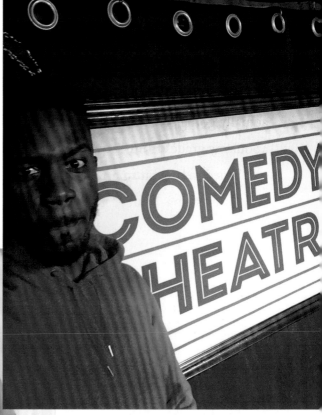

After my videos went viral, this was one of the shows where people started to recognise me.

Thank You
20k Followers

Hitting 20k followers on Instagram. This felt like a big milestone – little did I know what was to come …

but then I thought, *They're going to check!* I thought they were actually going to call AQA and Edexcel and find out I was lying about my grades from Year 6.

I tried to be a bit smart, though, because I didn't put that I got A* in everything. I put A* for science but threw in a couple of Bs too. All the while I was still thinking:

How is this going to help me fold clothes in retail, man? I'm applying to Debenhams!

But I knew that I had to follow the CV rules. The next section was the hardest to fill in. It asked me for my previous work experience.

Previous work experience? I've never had a job before! What experience am I gonna have, man?

I had read that you were supposed to end your CV with your hobbies and interests, so I put down that I liked playing football with my boys and 'chirpsing' girls on the weekend.

Chirpsing was a legitimate hobby for teenage boys, because we had nothing else to do but work on our game, which is what I did on weekends: go to Trocadero with the boys, see who could get the most girls' phone numbers, all the while trying our best to not get our phone robbed by a gang of youths.

If I was being honest, I'd have told those girls this: *Look, I'm NOT trying to phone you or get to know you. I just need numbers, as many numbers as possible, so that I look like the gyalist undisputed champion!* But, in reality, the only number we got was the number 12 bus home.

As I got more used to doing CVs, one trick that I used was to just say that I had worked somewhere in a certain year, rather than specifying dates like 'November 2006–January 2007'. That way, if employers checked and found out I'd only lasted two months there, I hadn't lied to them.

Even better was putting down places that had closed down, so they couldn't check. I put Woolworth's on there: I said I'd worked there for two years. I said that I had worked Christmas at Dixon's and followed up the lie in my Saturday job interviews, but it didn't always play out how I thought:

INTERVIEWER: So, it says here that you worked at Dixon's. When was that?

ME: Ah, I worked there when I was sixteen, just before it closed down. It's a shame!

INTERVIEWER: Yeah, it is a shame, the high street is changing. But it sounds like you have a lot of retail experi— Oh! You must know Alex, the area manager for Dixon's?

ME: Oh, yeah … maybe he left before I started?

INTERVIEWER: He? Alex is a lady…

When I took my CV into a shop, I learnt that the trick was to hand it direct to the shop's manager. They were the ones that were doing the hiring. I would go in and ask one of the assistants:

ME: Can I speak to the manager?

SHOP ASSISTANT: What's it for?

ME: I wanna hand in my CV.

SHOP ASSISTANT: Ah, you can give me it, I'll give it to them.

ME: No, do you mind getting them for me?

You'd have to be quite stern. Because actually meeting them might give you the chance to make a good impression.

You have to be prepared to print out twenty CVs knowing that nineteen will get chucked straight in the bin. But the other could be the one that gets you a job. That's how you need to look at it. But if you don't hear back within forty-eight hours, you won't normally hear anything. There's no point in waiting a week. You might as well just keep hunting. That lesson applies to life in general: don't stop and always keep going.

Some people go mad with their CVs. They put their photos on them, as if they are going for acting or modelling jobs, or they print them on coloured paper to make them stand out. I've seen people laminate CVs! That looks way too needy. Where did you even find a laminator?

Sometimes, applying for retail jobs online would be a total pain in the arse. I'd fill in loads of information on a complicated form and then at the end, it would say, 'Now upload your CV'.

What the fuck? Man just filled in six pages with information from my CV, and now you want to see my CV as well? And what's this you want – a letter of recommendation? Who from? Are you taking the piss, bruv?

Or they might ask you to answer three questions about random stuff, like what you want to achieve there. *What do I want to achieve? What I want to achieve is a decent wage so I can pay my phone bill.*

You're basically twerking for them for free and begging them to let you work there. *Like, come on! Cut me some slack, man! You're paying me minimum wage after all.*

I targeted specific shops that I wanted to work at, like Adidas, Foot Locker, Nike, Selfridges. Basically, it was all of the places where I wanted to be able to buy some decent clothes with a staff discount.

Even though you jump through all the hoops when you write out your CV, you get most of your jobs in your teens because one of your boys works there. A mate tips you that they're hiring, you give him your CV, they catch the manager for you, and *boom!* You're working there a week later.

It doesn't always work, though. One of my friends worked in a high-end clothes shop and told me they didn't even do anything and to top it off they got paid £9 an hour. *Man, £9 an hour!* He told me they got a good discount there, as well.

He said he'd give in my CV. I went in the shop secretly and just walked around, picturing myself working there. I wanted that job so bad ... but I never heard anything. I don't think my friend ever even gave my CV in, to be honest.

When I got out of college, I knew I had to start making money and take job searching a bit more seriously. So, I freshened up my CV, and it got me a job in Jo Malone at Westfield in White City.

That is a bit of a claim to fame for me: I started working in that Westfield on the day that it opened up. They were billing it as the biggest shopping centre in Europe. I was there on the grand opening day and it was mad. TV news crews were everywhere.

Jo Malone was in 'The Village', which is the really bougie part of the shopping centre, and I went along feeling smooth in my smart shoes, white shirt, black trousers and a really bait Zara mac (the white mac was long gone by then). I needn't have bothered. When I got there, this Trinidadian woman said, 'You just need to go in the stock room and move them boxes. Put an apron on.'

I was so pissed! *Fam, THIS is what I'm doing?* Plus, when I did get out on the shop floor, customers were being bare annoying and hood guys were walking past and laughing at me in my apron. Yes, I had to wear an apron to put out hand cream.

On that first day, Westfield were announcing that there were free goody bags in lots of shops. So, people were coming in, all excited, asking us, 'Have you guys got any freebies?'

'No.'

Jo Malone is pretty upmarket. And like a lot of upmarket shops, they don't put the prices on stuff. I would get the mandem coming in, asking, 'How much is this shower gel, bruv?'

'£30.'

'£30? Are you joking me?'

And a big part of me felt like saying, 'Yeah, it's crazy, innit?'

I always used to show customers one particular perfume that smells really good. It was the bomb. I showed it to so many people and they always wanted it. Then one day, one particular guy came in and we had this conversation:

CUSTOMER: This is nice, still. So, how long you worked here for?
ME: I've been here for a month.

CUSTOMER: So, if I steal this, will I get in trouble and that?

ME: Yeah bruv, you can't steal it.

CUSTOMER: Yeah, but if I steal it, are you gonna say anything?

ME: Nah I'm not gonna say anything, but, fam, allow it! Don't steal it!

(I was literally trying to negotiate with this guy while he was about to put it up his hoody!)

CUSTOMER: Man just wants to steal it. I'm not gonna lie, you know, bruv!

ME: I hear that, but allow it!

CUSTOMER: If I walked out of the shop with it now, what would happen?

ME: Bruv, I'm not gonna chase you!

CUSTOMER: *Walks straight out the shop with the perfume in his pocket.*

I thought about chasing him, but then I realised I'm not going to risk my life for a £50 bottle of perfume.

One day, Ian Wright came into Jo Malone. I didn't see him come in, but I was just restocking some scented creams and candles when one of my colleagues, Stuart, came over and said, 'Ian Wright's upstairs, bruv!'

Wow! Ian was such a childhood hero of mine. I loved the way he played – if I am honest, he was the reason that I started supporting Arsenal. I went upstairs to repack stock we didn't need, filling my basket with more scented candles and creams, just so that I could sneak a glance at him. As I walked past him queuing up at the checkout he saw me.

'You alright, man?' I managed to build up the courage to say.

'Yeah – what's happening?' he replied. We didn't really *talk*, not properly, but he was friendly. I was so gassed!

I went back down to the stockroom after I'd put out the candles and creams and had a freak out because Ian Wright had said hi to me.

The nice thing about working in retail was seeing guys that looked like me come into the shops I worked at and knowing I could help them. I'd always look after them, especially when it came to suits when I later started working at Reiss. I'd help them with alterations and give them a bit of a discount.

I worked in quite a few different shops after I left college and got quite good at being interviewed for retail jobs. I got most of the jobs that I went for. I didn't get all of them, though.

One time, I went for a job at Abercrombie & Fitch. A friend of mine was working there and he told me that they were hiring and it was a good place to work.

'Mo, it's cool, bruv!' he said. 'You know, they employ people just to dance?'

'*What?*'

'Yeah, we got a guy in the shop and all he does is dance about, with no shirt on! You should definitely try to work here!'

When I went down to see them, there were queues of people waiting outside the shop. *OK, cool!* But then, when I got inside, I realised that the good-looking staff were dancing, and those that weren't so good-looking were standing at the back, folding the clothes. That seemed a bit weird for me.

It was a group interview with other candidates but I had a good line prepared for it. When they asked me why I wanted to work there, I said:

'When I think of fashion, I want to look good. If I look good, I feel good, and that's what's great about Abercrombie & Fitch: you've got very stylish clothes, so if I was working here, I'd look good and feel good.'

After that, everyone in the interview who got asked the same question just remixed my answer! One girl said almost exactly the same as me and the interviewer was going, 'Good, great answer!' I couldn't believe it.

I didn't get the job.

• • •

Later in my life, when I'd started doing stand-up, I wanted to work in shops that were fairly quiet so I didn't have loads of people spotting me. My ego came into it as well: *Shit! I perform at the O2 – OK, it's the little Indigo club downstairs, but still!* I didn't want to be selling someone a T-shirt, and them to be going, '*Rah is that you? Yeah! Mo Gilligan!*'

But most people who recognised me were cool about it. They didn't laugh at me – they respected that I was earning a living. Now, I don't have as much of an ego like that as I did in my early twenties. I'll do whatever work it takes to pay the bills.

At the time, it felt like it was just me having to work multiple jobs in order to pursue my dream, but later on in life, I discovered a lot of my friends who are in the creative industry had to do the same.

During the years when I was trying to balance comedy and retail, I worked for a while in a shop called Thomas Pink, on Sloane Street, just up the road from Harrods. The shop was often dead so it was pretty boring, but the money was good.

I'd chat to my colleagues but the manager would get on my back: 'You're always talking! You've got to stop talking so much and get more focused!' *OK*, I thought, *fair enough, I'll cut back on the chatting.* I was still on my three-month probation period.

But one day, the shop was really empty, and I was standing by the door by myself. I'd just been offered a small TV role on a CBBC show, *The Johnny and Inel Show*, and I was running through a few lines in my head. That's when my manager came over to me.

MANAGER: You alright, Mo?

ME: Yeah, man.

MANAGER: What you thinking about?

ME: Nothing, I'm just thinking about a script.

MANAGER: OK, cool!

(Two weeks later, that guy called me into his office.)

MANAGER: I want to have a word with you.

ME: Sure. Wassup?

> MANAGER: You remember that time you told me that you
>   were thinking about a script?
> ME: Yeah.
> MANAGER: Well, I don't pay you to think about scripts in
>   your head! I pay you to serve customers.

Huh?

I went out of his office thinking, *There is something wrong with you, man. You have literally just told me that I'm not allowed to think!*

I think anybody who has worked in retail has at some point wanted to punch their manager in the face. You don't even have to be a violent person – I'm not – but you still fantasise about doing it. It's OK as long as it stays a fantasy!

That can be a problem with retail managers. I've had some really cool ones, but I feel like some of the managers I had maybe started out with hopes and dreams of their own and then somehow got stuck in retail. And they took it out on me. I could almost sense them, thinking: *Look at you with your hopes and dreams! No way, man! You need to come down here with me! Lose your aspirations and come down here into the pits, with me!*

One of the best places that I worked in my early comedy years was the Apple Store. I was only a sales associate, but it was a fun job. I got to meet a lot of like-minded creatives who had that job in the day, but pursued their own hobbies and passions at night.

I'm so glad that I worked in retail for a few years. It builds character and all walks of human life can be found there. We would get customers come screaming in, demanding a refund with no receipt on an item they bought six months ago. Well, what could I do except get my manager?

Retail teaches you about life and what makes us tick. I reckon people may come into shops to complain about a damaged item but, deep down, it's a complaint about something bigger in their lives. Sometimes, a stranger is the only person they can vent to, taking their anger out on a sales assistant on minimum wage, who they think represents the company. They often say the customer is always right, but sometimes there are exceptions to that rule.

Some customers are just dickheads.

6

THAT MOMENT WHEN ...

You Play Your Very First Gig

*L*et me be honest with you. I had never thought of doing stand-up comedy. It just hadn't occurred to me. I loved telling jokes to my mates, and making them laugh, but actually standing up on a stage? That felt like a whole other world!

My first experience of comedy was watching *Def Comedy Jam*. That was a big reference point for me. I loved watching young Black comics performing material in America to a young Black audience. They were talking to their peers, and making them laugh.

It wasn't big stars like Chris Rock. I saw upcoming, underground Black comedians like Bill Bellamy, Chris Tucker and Bernie Mac talking about things they maybe shouldn't have been talking about. It was all totally unfiltered – and it taught me a lot.

I don't just mean about comedy. It taught me about *life*. For example, I didn't know anything about the O. J. Simpson trial, as I was only six when it happened, till I saw them talking about it on *Def Comedy Jam*. It was watching that that made me realise how mad the case actually was.

Def Comedy Jam educated me on so many things I didn't know about in my teens and although it was comedy, it was a circuit where comedians could be unapologetically Black. It was a Black pop-cultural explosion. It was *Def Comedy Jam* that taught me how segregated American comedy was. I didn't feel like there was that same type of segregation here in the UK, even though Black comedians were, and still are, a minority in the stand-up circuit.

Def Comedy Jam helped me understand the landscape of America a little bit when they talked about a lot of social issues. As a teenager, I was just thinking, *Rah, this is funny!* – I used to laugh like crazy when I watched their DVDs – but now I realise that it was also educating me.

The great thing about watching *Def Comedy Jam* was that as much as it educated me, it was also introducing me to different comedians who had different styles and it certainly played a huge part in my early development as a comedian, even from a young age.

• • •

My first taste of seeing live stand-up had come when a friend of mine, Louis, asked me, 'Mo, there's a cool live show happening at Deptford Theatre – do you want to go and watch?'

It was a young Black comic called Slim and, man, he just blew me away!

We sat up in the balcony and I was crying with laughter the entire night. Slim was just so cool. He was effortless, telling jokes like he was talking to his best mate. I'd never seen him before but as soon as he walked onstage, Slim was totally relatable.

He had this persona about him that was just so likeable and everyone in the crowd loved him. It was like watching a UK version of *Def Comedy Jam*.

It wasn't a light-bulb moment, or like it is in the movies. I didn't go away knowing, *That's it! I want to be a comedian!* But I think, on a subconscious level, that Slim's show triggered something in me. It was a bit of a catalyst.

I still wasn't thinking of doing it myself, though – till one day, not so long after talking to a friend of mine from college, Tyrone, who'd told me that his aunty was about to get married, and out of the blue, he said to me:

'Mo, you're really funny. You should do stand-up. Would you wanna do some stand-up at this wedding?'

Wow! He took me totally by surprise and I didn't really know what to say. I could easily have bottled it and said no but I thought, *You know what? Let's try it!*

So, I told Tyrone, 'OK, I'll go for it! Let's give it a go!'

On the wedding day, I was feeling proper nervous. I remember worrying what to wear. In the end, I went in Air Forces, new trousers and a nice jumper – not too smart, not too casual. I got on the 63 to Elephant & Castle and nervously walked the rest of the way to the church, which was near Waterloo.

I had a small notepad with me that had a couple of jokes written in it and I kept scribbling in it. I didn't know how to start. In fact, I realised that I didn't really know the most basic thing of all: *how do you tell a joke?*

I was starting to realise that I wanted to perform, I wanted to make people laugh, but I didn't really have the first idea how to go about it. Plus, I knew I couldn't be rude or offend anyone, because … it was a wedding!

When I got there, it was a proper big Jamaican wedding. I noticed that Tyrone's mum had three or four sons and they were all really big guys, plus one daughter, who was quite small. So, when they asked me to do my bit, I made something up about them.

The wedding party were sitting, all in white, on a little raised stage. I was standing in front of it. I pointed at the girl and her brothers, and I said, 'Can you *imagine* when that girl first brings a boy home? Those dudes are going to be lining up to ask the poor guy questions:

'*Where you from? What time are you bringing our sister home? Make sure you look after our sister, yeah? You know what we'll do to you if you don't look after our sister?*'

If I'm honest, I didn't know where I was going with it, but people liked it and it got a few laughs. My whole five minutes or so was like that – I just looked around me, made a few funny (respectful) observations, and hoped for the best.

Looking back now, I can hardly believe that I dared even to do it, but I guess I was fearless at the time, like young people are. As I looked at the wedding party, who were all in white, I felt like we were in a medieval royal court and I was the jester performing.

If they liked me?

Yay! Great!

If they didn't?

Off with his head!

Actually, that's *not* exactly how I felt. I felt more like those people who go to Comic Con conventions and dress up as their favourite superheroes. They get to put on the cape and the boots and go 'Yay! I'm Superman!'

They know they're *not*, of course, but for that day, they're with people who let them feel like that. And that was what the wedding day felt like for me. I was with people who let me play at being a comedian. And it felt great.

It *was* great. The wedding guests laughed at all the right bits, and afterwards they told me 'Well done!' and invited me to stick around and have some food. Walking to Elephant & Castle Tube afterwards, I felt really pleased … and a little bit proud.

I had lost my comedy virginity, and I knew one thing: *Yeah! I could get used to this feeling.*

The funny thing is that now, years later, I won't do weddings. It's a very personal day and you can feel as if you are intruding on it. There are so many limits to what you can and can't say, and people are so picky because it's their big day.

The groom will ask you, often in a cockney accent, 'Can you do this joke about Dan, my best man? You won't get it and it won't make sense to you, but everybody will laugh.' Then you do the joke about Dan – and nobody laughs!

So, I've stepped away from doing weddings now, even though I've had one or two celebrities ask me to host theirs. It's just not my scene. But, at the time, Tyrone's aunty's wedding was exactly what I needed. It was great for me and it came at exactly the right time. It's like that famous phrase: when you wait for a bus and someone gives you a lift instead (OK, it's not a famous phrase, but it sounds good).

•   •   •

My second gig *was* at a proper comedy night. Round the corner from where I had grown up is a semi-professional, non-league football club called Dulwich Hamlet F.C. In fact, I knew their Champion Hill ground pretty well and after my family had moved to Peckham when I was sixteen, I got to know it even more.

In my mid-teens, I used to go to the ground with my mates and hang around the Astroturf football pitches watching the games. We'd be fifteen and asking the players, 'Do you guys need any subs?' Sometimes they'd be like, 'No, we're OK.' Other times, they might let us join in.

A family friend, Daveed, who used to work in the adventure playground when I was a kid, began booking the acts for the comedy events at Dulwich Hamlet. He usually booked singers, but he'd just started doing comics as well. He'd heard about the show I had done at the wedding and he gave me a call.

'Mo, I've booked two professional comics for one night next week,' he said. 'One is going to open up and host the evening, and the other is going to headline it. I've got space for a couple of new people in between, and I'd like you to do it.'

Wow! Cool! 'OK, great!' I said. And, inside, I was thinking: *Here we go!*

In the days leading up to the gig, I was writing down jokes in that same little notebook and practising my set in the bedroom mirror. When the time came, I put my joke book into my pocket and got the train one stop down the line to East Dulwich station.

I was still writing jokes on the train! When I got to Dulwich Hamlet F.C., I saw a few of my mates were there and had come down to support me. I was the guy in school who they all knew as the class clown, and now I'd told them I was gonna do comedy.

They were all like, 'Oh, man, this is gonna be wicked! You're so funny, you're gonna smash it onstage.'

It made me feel good that they were there to support me. But it also put pressure on me – *Shit! I've got to be funny to all these people! The ones that I know, AND the ones I don't know!* My head was all over the place and I kept having the same realisation: *It's a big day today! I'm doing a show!*

There was an MC hosting, who was the main guy. A comic was doing his set in the first half of the show, then there was a middle section for newcomers like me, doing five minutes each, then a headliner at the end.

I didn't know who the two main comedians were – but I was still in awe of them. *These are professional comedians! I'm on a bill with professional comedians!*

We were all hanging around backstage waiting to be called up onstage and the main man and the first comedian said hello to me. I couldn't believe they were even acknowledging me! But they were friendly:

'How's it going? You alright, man?'

'Yeah,' I managed to say. 'Nice to meet you.'

I told one of them that it was my first time and asked him if he could give me any tips. 'Just relax!' he said. 'Be yourself and you'll be fine!' I remember hoping that it was as simple as that.

I had been OK up till then, but now I started feeling the pressure. I was flicking through my joke book again when the MC wandered up to me and said, 'OK, you're on in one minute – you've got five minutes to do your set.'

Then, suddenly, I was walking out onto the stage, in front of the audience.

I walked out … and everything that I had written down and practised in front of the mirror went clean out of my head. Nothing. My mind went blank but, at the same time, in a funny way, it also cleared.

I can't remember what the first thing that I said was. It certainly wasn't one of the jokes that I'd carefully written down. I think I just said a random thing and maybe did a funny accent. But I noticed two things straight away.

The first one was that my voice didn't sound like me! I hadn't held a microphone on a stage and spoken into it before, and it made me sound different from normal. But I also noticed another, *far* more important thing.

People were laughing.

Wow! Just that instant hit, of me telling a joke and people laughing, was such a buzz: *People are laughing at what I'm saying!* I knew I had friends there, but I looked out into the crowd and I could see people I had never seen before all bussing up.

It was a totally new feeling … yet it was also everything I had ever hoped for.

What was I saying? I can't even remember. I think I was talking about going out raving. I was telling jokes, but they weren't the ones I'd written down beforehand. It was stuff I was just improvising, and going with, and everybody was laughing at everything. It felt like a dream.

I remember that I did a thing about getting on the bus in south London. I was talking about getting on, and how there is always an aunty with loads of shopping bags barging people out of the way. I started doing different passengers with different accents.

It segued into – and I was making this all up as I went along! – a thing about trying not to pay on the bus. I did the sound effect of the engine, then stopped it abruptly to do an impression of the driver as they're trying to see who hasn't paid. I could see my mates bussin' up ('bussing' up – ha!) and lots of strangers as well.

I had so much adrenaline pumping and I could feel that I had this huge, mad grin fixed on my face. I was smiling so much that I could feel my cheeks hurting. I could feel my heart beating like crazy, and my hands were shaking.

I was loving it.

I was supposed to do five minutes but I must have been up there for at least twenty. Eventually I said, 'Cool, man, that's my time – thanks a lot!' I got a nice round of applause: I was gassed about that. And I went off stage with my head in an even bigger whirl than when I had gone on.

It's so hard to describe how I felt when I got off. I said to myself, *Rah, shit! Man's done some stand-up!* But I wasn't really analysing it like that. I had one main thought, which was simply: *That. Went. Well.*

And it had.

It had gone better than I had thought, or even dared to hope, that it would. I didn't have a voice, or a style, as a comedian then. I didn't even really know what I was talking about. But I kind of realised: *I'm good at this.*

I came off and I stood to the side of the stage, and a lady who was going on next as the other new comic came up to me. She was being really kind. 'Well done, that was really good!' she told me. 'Have you done stand-up before?'

'No,' I replied. 'That was my first time.'

'Oh, wow!' she said. 'Cool!'

Then that kind lady went out for her turn … and she bombed. She *really* bombed. It was horrible to watch. I'd just got all this laughter, and she got absolutely nothing. I felt so sorry for the poor woman. It was her first time, too, and she looked like she wanted the ground to swallow her up.

I really felt for her … but, also, it made me realise even more how well I had just done. *I had proper made people laugh. Wow!*

I'm so pleased that I didn't bomb at my first real comedy gig, because if I had, who knows what would have happened? I like to think I'd have persevered, but maybe I'd have given up and decided it just wasn't for me. As it was, I just knew that I wanted to do more. So much more.

Let me tell you, that comedy event at Dulwich Hamlet F.C. will always have a very special place in my heart.

7

THAT MOMENT WHEN ...

Sunday Means The Sunday Show

*A*fter I made my comedy club debut at Dulwich Hamlet F.C., I started doing a few small, local gigs. I would enter talent shows and perform anywhere that I could. I didn't really know what I was doing: I didn't even have a stage name! I was just winging it.

Using my full name, Mosiah, didn't feel right. It just didn't have that presence, if you know what I mean. Having been inspired by *Def Comedy Jam*, I wanted a stage name that would feel like it rolled off the tongue, like Cedric the Entertainer, or Bernie Mac.

The name I settled on came about when I was performing at a little talent night in north London. Before I went on, the girl who was compering the night asked me, 'How do I introduce you?'

'I dunno,' I said, a bit lamely. 'Just call me Mo.'

'OK,' she said. Then, when it came time for my set, she went out onstage and said, 'Right, guys, now it's time for some comedy. We've got a guy called Mo, he does comedy… please welcome Mo the Comedian!'

When she said it, I liked the sound of it. From then on, I was Mo the Comedian.

• • •

Back then, I had a sort of stage style with regards to how I dressed. I'd always try to match things. If I wore red Vans, I'd wear a red t-shirt. Green Vans, a green t-shirt. I figured that it might help people to remember me!

There are some hideous pictures of me out there that only exist on a hidden folder on my Facebook. I remember having a pair of creps made from black tracksuit material with a pink tick and pink bottom. Bits of pink, all over the place. So naturally, I accessorised with a pink t-shirt.

Whose idea was that? Sadly, it was mine ...

At those early comedy shows, I always wanted to wear the freshest pair of creps I could onstage. It was a confidence-booster for me, in a subconscious way. Or maybe even a conscious one.

Those small local gigs reminded me of the DJ competitions in an old crime movie, *Juice*. Everyone on the scene knew each other. There was friendly competition, but we all encouraged each other.

One guy I became friendly with – and who I'm still friends with now – is James Massiah. James is a poet and we were always turning up on the same bills. His surname sounds like my first name, so people would ask us, 'Are you guys cousins?'

So, I was knocking around doing open-mic nights and talent shows, and I was happy to be out the house and getting gigs. Not only that, but the gigs were actually going well. It wasn't really on my mind to pursue comedy as a career. I was just enjoying myself.

Then, I got my big break. I discovered The Sunday Show.

The Sunday Show was a comedy show held every – guess when? – Sunday evening in the West End. A friend told me about it, and I tracked it down through their Facebook page.

It was held downstairs at a Slug & Lettuce bar in Soho. *The West End!* Even that was a big deal, to start with. Because so far, I hadn't got onstage anywhere in central London.

The Facebook page had a lot of photos, which gave me a chance to see what the audience was like. The crowd looked young and cool; I knew straight away that I wanted to perform there.

I couldn't have been any more nervous when I went down to Soho that Sunday afternoon. I found the Slug & Lettuce and followed the sound of the bass downstairs. At the entrance to the club was a girl with a clipboard, staring at her phone.

'Hi, you alright?' I greeted her. 'I'm performing tonight.'

She looked at me without a flicker of emotion, '*Are* you?'

Huh?

'Yeah, I'm performing!' I was so shy that I probably didn't sound very convincing. She clearly thought I was trying to pull a fast one and get in for free.

'OK, I'll text Marvyn, then,' she said, scrolling through the contacts on her phone. '*He'll* tell me if you're performing.'

I stood there awkwardly as she tapped her phone screen and a stream of paying customers filed past me.

Marvyn came to the door. He was a tall bald guy. It was his birthday – in fact, that week's The Sunday Show was billed as his birthday special.

'Marvyn, this guy says he's performing?'

He looked me up and down. 'No, he's got to pay £5,' he said, thinking I was a punter trying to blag my way in without paying.

'Oh, no, no,' I stammered. 'I messaged you on Facebook and you said to come down and do five minutes!' I couldn't believe I'd psyched myself for this set and now it might not even happen.

Marvyn still didn't look quite sure but he took my word for it and they let me in and showed me to a small, concealed area where the acts were waiting to perform. It was just a few sofas – basically a very low-level green room, or VIP area.

I could hear the DJ playing music in the main bar – all funky house, like Crazy Cousinz and Gracious K – but I was more excited by the fact that I was sitting with the *actual* performers.

Some big names had passed through The Sunday Show already, including Eddie Kadi and Paul Chowdry. Even Richard Blackwood had been down in the crowd.

I sat there nervously as the hosts, two comedians called Jamie Howard and Lee Littleman, performed to the crowd. They had them in the palm of their hands. Although this was great for the audience, it made me even more nervous. I could feel my palms getting sweaty.

Performing to your peers is like a double-edged sword. When it goes well, it goes well, but when it goes bad they'll be sure to let you know. They're judging you at every single moment, even down to the way you dress onstage.

From the side of the stage, I could look out on the crowd and I could see they were all young, wealthy creative types – or at least that's how they were dressed. Guys in Lyle and Scott T-shirts tucked into their True Religion jeans to show off their Gucci belts, and girls in Miss Selfridge dresses or wet-look leather leggings and heels with a full face of make-up on. Then there's me in my bootcut Blue Ink jeans – the ones that came with a free belt – swallowing up my shoes, getting ready to perform to these people.

When you're totally new to the game, like I was, your introduction is so dead because no one really knows who you are and you have no credentials for the comperes to announce to the crowd. I had watched so many *Def Comedy Jam* sets, thinking I was gonna get a big introduction like one of my heroes.

'Ladies and gentlemen, you're in for a treat tonight! This guy coming up to the stage, he killed it at Tyrone's aunty's wedding, and he's been smashing it recently at Dulwich Hamlets F.C. And now he's finally here! Put your hands together, go crazy, for the one, the only, MO THE COMEDIAN!'

The crowd goes wild and I have to tell them to sit down. 'Honestly, guys, you're embarrassing me!'

I wish that was how it happened, but it actually went a bit more like this:

COMPERE: Who's ready for some comedy?
AUDIENCE: *Silence.*
COMPERE: Well, get ready for some comedy! Here's Mo the Comedian!

And I walked out, in front of that big, hip crowd. Not just on the stage, but *through* the crowd, bumping people's shoulders as I squeezed past, mumbling, 'Excuse me, pardon me, coming through.'

I was so nervous, way more so than at Dulwich Hamlet F.C. I was holding the mic and literally trembling. Have you seen that funny meme of the guy drinking water and uncontrollably shaking? *That* was exactly what I looked like.

I started off with a routine where I was talking to an imaginary friend and doing both of our voices. It's an old joke that hasn't aged well and, to be honest, I think it's a bit shit now. But this is how it went:

ME: What's happened, man? Why are you crying?

FRIEND: It's nothing. I don't want to talk about it.

ME: No, come on, blud, it's upsetting me to see my friend crying like this. I'm your bruv. What's wrong?

FRIEND: I can't believe he's left. He's not in my life anymore!

ME: What do you mean? Who's left?

FRIEND: Ah, man, he was such a big part of my life! I feel like he grew up with me, there from my childhood!

ME: Shit! Who are you talking about?'

FRIEND: Thierry Henry! He's left Arsenal and gone to Barcelona! I can't believe it!

Like I say, I don't think that joke's all that great now, but it did get a good laugh from the crowd back then.

As I went on, the crowd continued to laugh at my jokes and the set was going well. I mean, I wasn't getting *huge* laughs, but a laugh is a laugh nonetheless and anything counts when you're onstage. If I am honest, I was surprised – I was used to my friends telling me I was funny, but making strangers laugh? That was something else!

I was just talking nonsense because I didn't have any life experience, really, but as I got the laughs, I could feel myself getting better. Laughter is contagious, even for the person onstage, and it gave me such a rush. It's been true all through my comedy career to date: the more confident I feel, the better I am at delivering the material.

As I stood there onstage, I felt my nerves just falling away. This was something I really wanted to do – why should I feel afraid? I loved the realisation that you have the power to improve someone's evening just through telling jokes. I knew in that moment I couldn't wait to perform at The Sunday Show again.

I'd found my calling.

The audience was five hundred mostly Black people, from all parts of London: north, south, east, west. I loved that it wasn't just some south-London thing. It was almost like a secret club. It was *the* place to be on a Sunday night, where you might see up-and-coming rappers from Channel U and SBTV.

The next set I got to perform at The Sunday Show was for a competition they put on called Yo Mama! – and what really caught my eye about it was that the winner would get £50.

I thought, *£50? It doesn't seem much to stand onstage with other guys and cuss each other's mothers – but I want it! I'm in!*

It was meant to be a four-way contest but a couple of comics had to pull out last minute, so it ended up being just me against another fairly new guy. Looking back on it, it was almost like we were gladiators being sent into the Colosseum, as everyone cheered us on to cuss each other's mums.

I knew the other guy was good, and yet I went into that contest feeling pretty confident. A modern-day Maximus Decimus Meridius, son of a single mother, brother of two sisters!

I always had a good arsenal of 'your mum' jokes at school, being the class clown. At break time we all used to roast each other, and I was that kid in the playground, with a small crowd around me laughing while I was bussin' jokes. I could really hold it when it came to a roast! I'm built for that stuff. *Let's have it!*

I spent a good week before the contest writing mum jokes. I had some killers, so I decided to go in heavy from the start ...

I loaded up the cannon of mum jokes and went straight in on this guy.

'Your mum's like a mosquito,' I told the other comic. 'I gotta slap her to get her to stop sucking!'

Crowd: '*Ooooh!*'

'That's raw!' I heard someone say.

He came back with something but it didn't get much response, so I went in deep.

'Blud, your mum's so dirty, when she takes off her knickers it sounds like Velcro!'

Crowd: '*Ooooh! He's taking no prisoners!*'

I looked around and could see everyone going wild. I was really going in hard on him. Even my opponent said, '*Rah*, bruv, you're going in!'

You know what, yeah, some of the cusses were a bit harsh. But, man, I wanted that £50!

This guy wasn't just taking it, though. He came back at me:

'Your mum's like a SIM card. She used to be a Virgin, now she's pay-as-you-go!'

Ouch!

He was clawing it back. 2–1 on the scoreboard. The crowd looked at me, waiting to hear what I'd come up with next. But I had a trick up my sleeve – or, rather, in my pocket.

The day before, I'd asked my girlfriend to do me a favour.

'Look,' I'd asked her. 'I need you to go to Ann Summers, or somewhere like that, and get some huge knickers – the biggest ones you can find.'

She did a wicked job. She came back with the biggest pair of knickers I'd ever seen. (They would hardly fit in my jacket pocket!)

I gave my opponent a *this-is-it* look.

'Look, I shouldn't really talk about your mum like this,' I said, as if I were ashamed.

The audience went quiet, like the crowd waiting for the winning serve at a tennis match.

'I shouldn't really disrespect her ...' I reached into my pocket and wrapped my fingers around the enormous knickers '... 'cause I was with her last night. Here are her pants!'

I pulled them out with a flourish and dangled them in the air. Those huge pants. Everyone went absolutely crazy. *'Aaaah!!'* They were laughing and bussin' up. I'll never forget that reaction.

Finally, I had that Def Jam moment I'd always wanted.

I won and with that £50 I took a couple of my mates to one of the touristy pizza places around Piccadilly Circus and bought us all dinner. They were nearly buzzing as much as me. I still remember one of them, Louis, telling me, 'I really feel like this is your time, bruv. I feel like this is gonna work out for you.'

I didn't know what to say back. I didn't know if he was right – it seemed too much to hope for. All I knew was that I was loving doing stand-up more than I'd ever loved doing anything.

I had one impulse: *Oh my gosh, people are giving me money to do what I love! I want to wake up and do this every single day!*

After that, I got the pass to go to The Sunday Show and be part of the team. Once I'd done a few shows, Marvyn said to me, 'You're family now, Mo! Come in whenever you want!'

That felt wicked! In fact, Marvyn did far more than that. He asked me if I wanted to host The Sunday Show every week. *Shit – of course I did!*

Then, one day, he took me out for lunch, sat me down, and had a serious proposition for me.

'Look, I'd like to help you,' he said. 'I'd like to be your manager. If anyone asks you to do gigs for them, you can just give them my email.'

Boom! So suddenly I had a manager! Marvyn managed me for a couple of years, but he never took any money at all. He never took a cut from anything but just mentored and helped me to not get ripped off by people and to understand my worth when it came to booking jobs.

What a guy! And let me tell you, Marvyn got involved at just the right time for me. He was one of the first people who let me know my worth. And at that stage of my development, and my career, that was crucial for me.

Once I started hosting The Sunday Show every week, it was a proper training ground to develop as a comic. I got to perform to 500 people every week and I got to try different things out. It was proper trial and error – some worked great, some not so much. I learnt as I went along.

What was nice was I started becoming aware that some people were coming down specifically to see me. They knew I'd be there every week and I'd occasionally hear people saying, 'Rah, I'm here to see you, Mo!' That was lovely and it meant a lot.

Sometimes it could feel like hard work. Some weeks we didn't have a big-name headliner, and I'd have to carry the show: be the host, make people laugh, introduce the musicians. But those often turned out to be the best shows. I'm not tooting my own horn here, but I think when you're responsible for a lot, needing to step up, whatever it is, you make the best of it, and I did.

Afterwards, people would be saying to me, 'You're sick, Mo! You're good at this!' That was a real driving factor for me, in the same way that Miss Simpson telling me I was good at acting. It motivated me.

Some weeks we had great people on. I got to introduce Slim, the comic who had blown me away at Deptford Theatre. He had just appeared on *Kojo's Comedy Fun House* and his episode was constantly being repeated on MTV Base and was all over YouTube. He was becoming a household name.

Slim being at The Sunday Show was a real incentive to me to be on top form. I did a fifteen-minute set before he came on and I was trying so hard to be funny that night, because I knew how great he'd be when he came on! I think, most of all, I wanted to show him: *Hey, Slim,* I'm *pretty good as well!*

It was a real thrill for me to introduce him and after I did, I just stood off in the sidelines and watched the master at work. He was just as great as he'd been at Deptford Theatre.

I got to talk to Slim afterwards and he was a really warm guy. Some older comics would take it upon themselves to give me advice. As much as I appreciated it, sometimes it felt like they were just telling me to do what they had done, as if there was only one way to do comedy.

Slim wasn't like that. He just said, 'What's up, Mo? I love what you're doing. Very funny. Keep it up.' He was very genuine and told me to big myself up. I was simply buzzing off the fact that he knew who I was, and what my name was!

•   •   •

I was performing every single Sunday for a whole year. The only Sunday we wouldn't do The Sunday Show was Christmas Day, but then we'd be back on Boxing Day. And we'd still pull in an audience of five hundred people.

The Sunday Show was the place to be. It was wicked. Footballers and musicians, or grime MCs like Skepta, would come down. You didn't normally see MCs at comedy nights so that was a big deal. Ed Sheeran even dropped in. Some people came once; others every single week.

I was *always* there. Every Sunday. I missed family birthdays, Mother's Days, Valentine's Days, so many things, because I was the main host.

The Sunday Show got bigger and over the course of a year it moved from the Slug & Lettuce to another bar called Strawberry Moons. Eventually we moved into a big nightclub called Sound. That was a big deal. Despite all the great stuff and the fact that we were moving into bigger venues, some real goons came down there! Like, I'm talking *serious* guys. And they'd tell me that I was funny: 'Hey, Mo, you're actually really funny! Keep doing your ting, bro!' they'd advise.

It was the equivalent of Joe Pesci from *Goodfellas* going to a comedy show and telling the comedian after he's come off stage that he thought he was funny.

Sometimes, these goons of Goonchester would even order me drinks:

'Get my guy Mo a double Hennessy on the rocks, you feel me?'

I normally have a rule that I don't drink when I'm performing, but with these sorts of guys, when you get offered a drink, you don't refuse it.

Like I say, we performed week in, week out to five hundred people. It got to the point where not everybody could get in because the place was that packed. People would travel all the way in to get told 'we're at capacity, you can't go in.'

I'd arrive and get escorted past all the disappointed people who had trekked into the West End on a Sunday and couldn't get in. I felt sorry for them – but I also felt like The Man!

I hosted The Sunday Show for two years but I left because I wanted to explore more of what comedy had to offer. I had tried out a lot of new things in my time there and grown a lot as a comic, but I could sense that it was starting to become a bit too easy and that I needed to push myself to take on the next challenge.

It was a big decision for me. The Sunday Show days were an amazing time in my life. It was my introduction to proper stand-up. It gave me the skills to entertain a crowd – skills I still use to this day – as well as a steady income and friends for life. I loved my time there dearly and I will never forget it.

But it was time to branch out.

8

THAT MOMENT WHEN ...

You Can't Afford the Train Fare to Your Shows

While I was playing The Sunday Show every week, I met loads of great Black comedians about the same age as me. They'd all come down to perform. There was Babatunde Aléshé, who was huge on the Black circuit back then, Travis Jay, Aurie Styla, Jazzie Zonzolo, Axel Blake and London Hughes (or Miss London, as she went by in those days).

There was also A Dot Comedian, who had these great sketches that everybody knew. A Dot was from Peckham, so me and him had a bit of a connection. We also had Kevin J. He was a little ahead of the rest of us – he'd normally headline, because he'd done an amazing set on a comedy show on *MTV Base*.

I met KG Tha Comedian and Nicholas Marston at The Sunday Show when they were doing some filming at the back of the audience. This was before they became Shadrack and the Mandem and did that video where KG was on roller skates which went viral and got them known.

I was hosting on the day they came down, and I had a chat with KG and Marston. They were after advice that might help them to break through: 'What can we do?' I was asking myself the same question at the time, but I tried to give them a few tips.

That was how it was on the Black comedy circuit then. If you had any advice that might help people, you shared it around.

Because there weren't many places that Black comedians could go. Nobody was getting any TV work. *Nobody*. The best you could hope for was going on Tim Westwood's radio show on Radio 1Xtra, which in a way was bigger than TV, because people would hear the comics who came on and then watch their clips on YouTube.

But you didn't see anybody who looked like you or sounded like you on TV. Just the occasional musician. I remember when Tinie Tempah started going to number one and found mainstream success. We were all like, *Woah! Look at Tinie – he's gone clear!*

That was the phrase you heard all the time: *Gone clear!*

When Tinie went to number one with 'Pass Out', he had a celebratory party across the road from The Sunday Show. Me and Marvyn stopped by. I remember seeing a couple of famous faces, and Tinie's crew throwing him up in the air. I just thought, *Wow! Look at this success, man!*

Going number one back then was even tougher than today, so this was a very big deal in UK Black music. It was crazy for me to see a young Black man being celebrated like that, in a West End club no less. I didn't know Tinie personally, but I found myself feeling so happy for him. I felt like I was witnessing a historic moment in the entertainment industry; you could practically hear the walls breaking down for other young Black artists to reach the same level of success. It inspired me.

After deciding to leave The Sunday Show behind, I knew that I wanted to do other things. I wanted to take my comedy as far as it could go and play to every type of audience out there.

The only thing that I *didn't* know was how to begin to go about it.

Comedians would talk about taking their careers mainstream. But what did that really mean? From what I could see, the mainstream comedy circuit was pretty much the same as the Black comedy circuit, except that the venues were more established, like Comedy Store or Up the Creek.

There didn't seem to be an obvious route to playing them. A lot of comics on the Black circuit felt that White audiences might not get what they were talking about, so it was best to not even try. For some comics those gigs also felt like a step backwards, because even if you were a big deal on the Black circuit, the promoter at one of these clubs might put you on first because he wouldn't have heard of you. But, by now, I also felt that I had a lot to offer in comedy and I wanted to try to play everywhere that I could.

So, I started doing a few open-mic nights at various pubs. I entered the Laughing Horse New Act of the Year Competition, which was a contest that gave new comics more exposure. I got through the heats but was knocked out in the finals. Still, that was OK – and at least I had made a different crowd laugh!

I also started trying to get gigs in other parts of the country. Honestly, I didn't know where to begin. I was literally going on Facebook and asking anyone if I could perform and maybe get paid £20 for it. I never even thought to ask for travel expenses.

Travel expenses? What are they? I just figured that £20 should get me there and get me home. That was about as far as my thinking went. I started sending out messages to pubs and universities that held comedy shows, asking them if I could come down and perform.

I was barely getting by, which made it a bit mad. I would ring up and get myself a gig at a little comedy club somewhere like Sevenoaks in Kent. They'd say they'd give me £40 and I'd set off there with my iPad in my little backpack and, at most, £20 in my pocket.

The train ticket would take £10 of that. I couldn't afford taxis, so I'd have to walk to the venue – Google Maps was my friend (even though my phone always seemed to be on 10% battery!). And I knew that I'd have to catch the last train back to London because there was no way I'd have enough for a B&B for the night.

So, I'd be performing, and making people laugh, but always with that last-train time in the back of my mind. After I'd finished my set, I'd be talking to the promoter. He might be saying, 'That went really well – thanks for coming down! We'd love to book you again!' And I'd chat with him, but then I'd have to be really uncool, and say, 'Thanks! Er ... can I get paid?'

He'd say, 'Yeah, sure! Just give me a minute!' Then he would get distracted and start doing something else, and I'd be quietly panicking: *Oh, bruv! You're eating into my time here! I need to get this last train!*

When I did *finally* get paid, the last train would probably be due in ten minutes – and I'd be fifteen minutes from the station!

So, I'd have no choice but to run there. I did a lot of unwanted late-night jogging. My comedy career was keeping me fit!

I would find myself in Birmingham with only £50 from the gig in my pocket. I'd want to get the fast train home but couldn't afford it – I'd have to go on the slow train, which felt like it stopped a thousand times. Or risk a nervy journey on the fast train with my cheaper ticket and hope for the best. Sometimes, jobsworth inspectors would catch me, and I'd have to spend all the money I'd just earned for the gig – and more – putting a full-fare ticket on my already overspent credit card (kids, don't ever get a credit card).

When I got back to London after midnight, I'd get the last Tube or, more often, walk to Kings Cross, then get the 63 back home to Peckham. I'd fall into bed at two o'clock. And I'd usually have work in a shop the next day – before another gig that same night.

Often, I simply couldn't afford the train fare to get to the gigs. I would have to hustle. I'd go on a selling spree and start selling my old creps on eBay or Depop. They were like my unofficial tour sponsors!

One guy showed me a life-saver hack on the trains. He said if I missed my train out of London, I should go onto London Underground's website and see which stations were closed or lines were delayed. Then I could get to Euston, or wherever, go to the ticket office and say that I had missed my train because my Tube got delayed. He said then they'd let me use the ticket on the next train.

It worked!

I missed one mainline train by three minutes and asked an inspector if I could use my ticket on the next train instead. He looked doubtful but he took me to the ticket office. I had checked online and I knew that Kew Gardens Tube station was shut. (Who the *hell* lives in Kew Gardens?)

'Can I get the next train, please?' I asked the ticket-office guy, showing him my ticket. 'It's just that my Underground station was closed, innit, so I had to go an alternative route that made me late.'

'Where have you come from?'

'Kew Gardens.'

The guy checked his screen ...

'Ah, OK. Can I check your Oyster card?'

'Er, I didn't use it – I did it on my debit card ... '

He bought it.

'Ah, OK, pass me your ticket ... '

He stamped it – STAMP! STAMP! STAMP! – 'Permission to travel.'

'There you go!' And he handed my ticket back.

Man got on the next train! *Oh my gosh!* I was so gassed! I was using an off-peak ticket for £43, my almost-dead phone charging on the seat next to me. I'd have had to pay £85 to get on the next train. And I just didn't have that sort of money.

• • •

At this stage, I was still working in retail during the day, playing gigs in the evening and managing my career myself. I still had Marvyn in my corner, of course, but he'd always been more of a mentor than a manager, and in those days I'd become pretty self-sufficient at booking my own work. But I'll admit, it was starting to become a lot to do just on my own.

Just through knowing someone, I got offered a short acting job on CBBC called *The Johnny and Inel Show*. It was there I met a producer called Polly, who I later discovered had cast me for the role. I found out Polly had just set up her own agency, UTC Artist Management, with her husband, Geli, and was representing a few people I knew. We got on great – and I asked her if she would manage me.

'I don't really know what I'm doing,' I admitted to her. 'I feel like I'm just making it up as I go along. Can you help me?'

It was the first time I'd ever voiced that I needed help. I was a classic twenty-year-old who thought they don't need anyone but themselves. But juggling so many jobs had put me at breaking point.

Polly said she'd think about it. About a month later she called to tell me that she and Geli would do it together. *Rah!* Asking her had been pure gut instinct, but it worked out so well. Those guys are still managing me to this day.

• • •

When Polly and Geli took over, they found me some cool gigs. One time, I got booked to play Camp Bestival, down in Dorset. Bestival is the full-on, late-night, wide-eyed music festival, while Camp Bestival is the younger-brother version for families and kids. Polly said some of the kids might have seen me on CBBC.

I wasn't that keen.

The show was at midday on a Sunday and I didn't even know how I could get there. Trains to Bournemouth were mad expensive, there weren't any on Sunday mornings anyway, and no way could I afford a hotel the night before!

On the Saturday afternoon, I was still in bed and on the phone to Polly, telling her I couldn't make it and I didn't want to go. I thought she'd have sympathy and pull me out of the line-up, but instead she matter-of-factly told me the next train to Dorset left at six o'clock, then she helped me book a B&B for that night in Bournemouth. And before I knew it, I was en route to a show I couldn't be arsed to do, but I guess beggars can't be choosers.

The festival organisers said I had to be there two hours before my set, so that Sunday morning I was up stupid early to get a little train from Bournemouth to the festival. When I got there, I was given my wristband and went in to find everyone fast asleep in their tents.

I located the stage I was performing at and introduced myself to the stage manager:

'Hi, I'm Mo! I'm performing today at twelve o'clock!'

'Are you?' she asked. She checked her running order and seemed very surprised to see me there so early.

'Oh, OK, you can wait in here!' And she put me in a little tent for two hours, which had folding tables and loads of flies buzzing around.

When it got to midday, I went on and started doing my set, but it wasn't going like I hoped. The kids weren't getting it at all.

The mums and dads behind them were laughing, but the kids were all looking at me like, *Huh? What are you on about?*

I wasn't at all sure what I should do, so on a whim, I asked all the kids, 'Do you know what my favourite song is?'

'No!' they all said.

'My favourite song is "Gangnam Style"!'

The second that I said it: *They. Lost. Their. Minds!* The kids were all going wild! So, I asked the stage engineer to put the song on, and I asked the kids, 'Who wants to do the best "Gangnam Style" dance?'

Man, they were fighting to get up there! The stage had a sort of catwalk, and these kids were all going crazy dancing up and down it to 'Gangnam Style'! All I had to do was say, 'Wicked, man! How good is *he?*' and choose the next kids to come up:

'Yeah, you can come and have a go! And you, as well!'

So that show went well in the end, even though it had absolutely nothing to do with comedy! I was just having fun and having a laugh.

• • •

By now, I was doing all sorts of shows. I performed in pubs up and down the country. I even performed at Eritrean Independence Day! Anywhere there was jokes to be had, I was there.

Of course, not every show went well. I remember performing at another kids' festival in Oxford. I was in a huge tent that would have held hundreds but there were probably ten people there. Most of them were stewards.

There was only one child, with his mum and dad. I went on and said, 'What's up, kids? Oh – it's just you!' That didn't even get a smile! Then I was doing my routine about how mums dance and didn't even get a laugh then. I was thinking, *This is my low point ...*

• • •

I was still grinding away in retail, running up and down the country doing shows but then, in 2015, I did a super-important thing that taught me so much. It is without doubt one of the most significant things I've ever done as a comic: I started my own comedy night.

I had a few reasons for doing this. One is that I'd noticed promoters were the ones who made the money out of comedy shows. And fair enough, they're the ones who get things started, take the risks and book the venues ... but I wanted to cut out the middleman, basically.

When I was doing The Sunday Show, I used to scrutinise every detail. I used to look closely at when people turned up, where they used to sit, what they liked and what they didn't. Sometimes I'd see new people come who maybe weren't used to how comedy nights work, and they might be saying, 'Oh – it hasn't started yet! It says eight o'clock on the tickets and now it's 8.15!'

The Sunday Show taught me stuff about how to look after people and it was crucial to me that we got everything right for my comedy night.

I mean, ideally, I wanted to tour – but I was nowhere near that level yet, and often wondered *Will I ever be?* So, in the absence of that, I wanted something that felt like mine, and so I started getting the wheels in motion.

I began by looking for venues. Initially I was just trying places I had played before, in the Shoreditch or maybe Kings Cross area. Most of them were just bars with a downstairs room they might use at weekends but were normally empty during the week.

It made sense to me to do it in Shoreditch because it was cheaper, had a younger crowd, and loads was happening there. There were comedy nights, poetry nights, music nights, you name it. It was important to me to be part of this creative hub.

Shoreditch had been through the mad hipster phase – maybe it was still going through it! – of guys in red trainers, skinny jeans, checked shirts and Nike blazers. But it felt like a happening place. If we were lucky, we might pick up some passing trade; 'What's this, a comedy night? Cool, let's have a look!'

So, I set my sights on E1 and started working the phone.

ME: Hello! I was wondering what you do with your downstairs room on a Tuesday night?

VENUE MANAGER: We don't do anything with it.

ME: Cool! Is it possible to use it for a comedy night?

VENUE MANAGER: Yeah, sure.

ME: Great! So, how much would that cost?

VENUE MANAGER: £2,000, plus VAT.

Woah! Hold on there! But that was nearly always the initial response from owners. I'd think to myself:

You don't do anything with the room on a Tuesday! It's earning you nothing! If I do my comedy night, I'll be bringing in maybe a hundred or two hundred people who'll be spending money in YOUR bar. You'll make a lot of money off them ...

But then I got lucky when a place called the Bedroom Bar, upstairs from the Comedy Café, said they'd let me do a trial on a Tuesday night. In between folding shirts in my day job, I started putting a show together.

I wanted to put on a comedy night that was *by* comedians and *for* comedians. By then, I knew a load of comics and I knew it was important to pay them fairly.

It was just me trying to get things moving, together with a friend called Emmanuel, who helped me out. I called the night Cracking Up Comedy, nervously put some tickets up for sale online and started trying to publicise the night on Instagram and Facebook, but I knew that wouldn't be enough.

I used to see *Time Out* magazine being handed out free when I walked past the Tube station. I contacted them and they put me in their listings and 'Things to Do in London' feature. I did the same with a couple of comedy blogs.

Getting comics to perform wasn't too hard. They might all be busy on Friday, Saturday and Sunday nights, but not on a Tuesday or a Thursday. I'd just call them up:

'Hey, what's up? I need a favour. I'm doing this little show on a Tuesday – can you do a ten-minute set for £50 for me?'

'Sure, man!' they'd say. 'I can do that.'

YOU CAN'T AFFORD THE TRAIN FARE TO YOUR SHOWS

The first show was mad because I'm such a control freak that I was running around trying to do everything. I was selling the tickets, doing all the online stuff, hosting the show – if I could have worked the door as well, I would have! I knew that if it went wrong, I wanted it to be on *my* shoulders, not anybody else's.

Doing a free show was not an option. I knew we had to sell tickets, because that was the only way I'd be able to pay the other comics. I kept checking the website: *Only 50 tickets sold! Oh, come on, man!* But then, luckily, there was a big influx of sales two days before our first night.

I loved that.

Today, now that I have a name, I can put tickets on sale for a show and they will sell out instantly, but back then it felt like people were buying tickets just because they might know me from The Sunday Show and they wanted to see some comedy. It might sound weird, but it felt *pure*.

A mate of mine came down to DJ. He started spinning tunes real early because I'd told him I wanted the event to start as soon as the doors opened, whether there was one person in there or a hundred. This was important to me because I wanted people to feel they were getting good value for their money. Those are the audience members who will come back week after week.

The first Cracking Up Comedy went really well. We got well over a hundred people in, I put on four comics who all went down great. The venue's management were pleased with the turn-out and profits, and I knew I was going to do more.

I started putting on the night once a month. After that first show, I became more business savvy and played with the tickets online. I sold early-bird and two-for-one tickets. I even started doing VIP tickets for £15. Some people just like being VIPs! Those tickets went down a treat for people taking a date. These guys would have seats reserved for them when they got to the show. They'd know they could come a bit late, maybe straight from work, and they'd be just fine.

The funny thing was, of course, I was still working during the day – I was at Reiss at this point – during the first few Cracking Up Comedy nights. I'd have to ask my manager for the night off:

'Oh, I'm doing this comedy night on Tuesday. Can I swap my shift?'

'Yeah, sure. You'll have to work on the Sunday. Hope your little comedy thing goes well!'

I could tell they thought it was just me and a few mates messing around; they had no idea I was getting two hundred people down each time. But that was OK. I mean, most of my colleagues didn't know me outside of work.

I did Cracking Up Comedy month after month and it kept getting better and the shows got bigger. Initially the management there were a bit uptight. At one of the early shows, we were playing music loud before the first comic went on and the manager came downstairs.

'Can you turn it down?' he asked me. 'It's not a nightclub!'

'Eh? It's a Tuesday night, and there are no residents around here!' I said.

But we were getting people in and when the manager saw the money rolling in from the bar spends, he soon stopped complaining. Instead of 'not a nightclub' it was, 'Sure, crank it up, man! Do you want to do more nights?'

Bedroom Bar was a good place for us to start and we had some great nights there, but after a few months the managers of the Ace Hotel, a trendy boutique hotel across the road, called me up. They invited me across and showed me a swanky nightclub they had downstairs called Miranda.

'Mo, we love what you do!' they said. 'We've seen you over the road and we want you to bring your show here!' They were totally cool from the off and they made me a very attractive offer.

The manager said, 'If you come here, you can keep the ticket sales and we'll keep all the bar take.' I loved that! It was a perfect partnership, and it was very fair. I knew they'd make more on the bar than if I gave them, say, 20% of the ticket sales. Everybody wins!

I wasn't making a load of money from Cracking Up Comedy, but … *boom!* It felt special because I was just about getting by doing what I wanted to do. It felt amazing: *This is mad! I'm actually making money from what I love now!*

I can't tell you the feeling of when you earn a wage and it's through what you love doing. That money felt different from the money I was earning folding shirts and negotiating with thieves. It felt more *real*. When you are working in a job that you don't particularly like, you tend to think:

I'm going to fucking blow this, man! I'm going shopping. I'm gonna go out this weekend! I'm probably gonna get drunk!

You don't even care about it. But when you make money from your passion, you actually have care for that money. You're thinking, *Whoa, I've earned this doing what I love. How can I re-invest this back into myself and fund the dream?*

Of course, running the night came with its own stresses and pressures. I'd get headline comics cancelling at the last minute, or turning up on the night and saying, 'I've got another show across town – can I go on first?' and I'd have to get someone else to fill in.

But it was all worth it. Putting on a comedy show for comedians taught me the art of producing a great show. It also taught me that if you want something done right, you have to do it yourself (and with a little help from your friends).

• • •

Cracking Up Comedy was going great. That didn't mean that everything in my career was as successful. Far from it! I had a major disappointment when I entered a competition to try to get to the Edinburgh Festival.

The festival organisers were putting on contests that were like auditions for the winning comics to play a well-known space at The Fringe. My audition was in Nottingham. All train tickets from London cost £80 except for one at two o'clock, which was £20. (*Looks like we're back on the cheap train again.*) Boarding this earlier train meant that I was in Nottingham four hours before I was due to play, so I sat in the pub where my audition was being held, nursing a lime and soda, and trying to look busy on my laptop, when the barman wandered over.

'You here for the comedy show, then?'

'Yeah.'

'You're a bit early!'

Yeah. Thanks for telling me that, buddy! Just keep bringing them lime and sodas over …

The show was in the pub cellar so, when it came time to start, I went downstairs to see the technician. The main part of my set had music throughout and I'd lined it up on my iPad with a jack so the guy could plug it into their sound system. I explained to him how it worked.

'It's the first track on my iPad,' I said. 'Just press play. That's all you have to do.' I could tell the guy was only half-listening when he nodded at me.

Although the show was effectively an audition, it was open to the public, but at seven o'clock it hadn't filled up. There were only about eight people there. I wasn't too worried because I was meant to be on in the second half, but then the organiser pulled me aside.

'I'm sorry about this, but the other comics are running late so we're going to put you on first,' he said. 'Is that OK?'

Hmm.

I never like going on first, but as it was an audition and I could hardly tell him no, I said, 'Yeah, cool!' And I got up onstage in front of the Edinburgh bookers and eight paying customers in that poky cellar.

I told my first joke. I can't remember what it was, but that's probably because I'm in denial and have blanked it out, because not a single person laughed. *Not. A. Soul.* You could have heard a pin drop.

Still, I was about to go into my big musical number. Maybe that would turn things around! *Here goes ...*

'Have you ever noticed when you go out raving, and all the guys are over on one side of the dance floor and the girls are on the other?' I asked. 'DJ – play that track!'

I nodded at the technician. He nodded back at me. And then did nothing.

Silence.

'Er, can you play that track, please?' I asked him, into the mic.

'Play a track? Sure!' And then he pushed a button and started playing some music of his own!

'No, no, no, no, no, no!'

I had to go over to him. 'Brother, I asked you to play the first track on my iPad!' I told him.

'Oh!' the technician said. He pressed it straight away and the track started, even though by now I wasn't even on the stage!

Fuck! I had to stop it, go back to the stage and ask him to start it again. Of course, all this had killed the joke stone dead. My next joke had music in it as well and went down just as badly.

Nobody. Was. Laughing.

I was used to audiences at The Sunday Show and Cracking Up Comedy, where people were falling about at everything I said, and now I was stuck in this empty cellar in Nottingham with eight people and nobody even cracking a smile.

Man, it was a disaster! At the end, I said, 'Cool, cheers, thanks a lot, guys! Have a great evening!' I thought maybe it was just a shit audience – but then all of the comics who went on after me were getting laughs. So, I couldn't even blame that.

I couldn't have felt any more shit. Polly texted me to ask how it had gone. I sat in the audience of eight people and typed out my answer.

> It was the worst gig I've ever had. Maybe I should just become a drug dealer, or something, because I don't think I want to do this comedy stuff anymore.

To make things even worse, I missed the last train to London and had to get a lift back with some of the other comics. Now, road trips with comics who you *know* are fun. They can be the best thing about gigs outside of London. But road trips with comics you *don't* know – man, that can be awkward.

There were five of us crammed into this little car, a red three-door. For some reason, the driver had decided to make the entire journey while tootling along in the slow lane. We seemed to keep having the same conversations about comedy.

'So, anybody going to any shows in Edinburgh this year?'

Man! I really, really, REALLY did not want to be in there talking about everyone's upcoming shows. I knew I would *not* be going to Edinburgh that year, so didn't want to hear any more about it.

The beautiful thing about comedy, though, is that after you have a bad gig like that, you can very quickly have a good one. That sort of gig helps you to grow a thick skin. You just have to have the confidence to pick yourself back up again.

Well, you try – but you can't always do it.

This period, while I was still working in retail, juggling comedy and trying to break into the mainstream, was hard for me. I couldn't see a light at the end of the tunnel. If I got a headline gig, which was rare, it was usually because the last comic to perform had dropped out and I'd become the headliner by default.

I still felt like my material was good and I was doing OK shows, but I wasn't the guy that everyone was coming to see. I was plodding along, sure, but it seemed like I had hit a creative brick wall.

I started running into money trouble. I was always skint and had mates saying, '*Rah*, Mo, we're thinking about going to Ibiza or Miami, do you wanna come?'

I'd tell them I had shows coming up, or was planning on going to Edinburgh, because I was too embarrassed to say I couldn't afford it.

It can be easy to let these things get on top of you. I'd got a credit card for emergencies, to help me get to gigs and stuff. But then some months a show I'd been waiting on would get cancelled and I ended up using it to pay my rent. That was always a bad, weird feeling – *What am I supposed to use to pay back the credit card people?*

Sometimes, I'd end up borrowing money from payday lenders. The interest rate on a credit card was bad enough. Meanwhile, these lenders' rates were in the *thousands*. I got caught in a vicious cycle of borrowing from one source to pay off the other.

It was manageable but it was still debt. I might owe a grand on my credit card, the same to a lender …

I knew that between retail and comedy on the side, I should be able to earn a decent wage. But some weeks I did and some weeks I didn't. I'd be folding shirts, or on the train to a show, and just doing money sums in my head. All the time.

That shit gets you down, and it got to the point where I wasn't even enjoying the gigs quite as much. It was like: *Am I doing this just to get the moneylenders off my back? Or because I love it?* It was all taking up too much head space …

The good thing was that Cracking Up Comedy was going from strength to strength at its new home, the Ace Miranda. I can't deny it, though – it was difficult to balance everything. Running up and down the country on trains that I could hardly afford just to play badly paid shows, managing my own comedy night, trying to keep the credit-card people and moneylenders happy, while slumming it in retail to try to make ends meet.

Breaking through to the mainstream wasn't happening any time soon, and I couldn't really see a way through.

But then I started uploading a few videos …

9

THAT MOMENT WHEN ...

You Go Viral and Stop Selling Jeans

Drizzy ✅ followed you

When I was starting out doing stand-up comedy, I got small levels of what I like to call 'hood fame'. Basically, you're kinda known in the hood but it's not *fame*, if that makes sense. People would just come up to me and say things like, *'Oh, rah, you're Mo? I've seen you before. Keep up the good work!'* I guess rappers have the same thing. You might get recognised when you go to the barbershop. It's just hood fame, in your local area and your ends, and there's nothing wrong with that. It's very pure and sincere.

In fact, hood fame means a lot. Getting recognition from where you're from means the world. You walk up and down your high street, and someone says, 'Oh, you're Mo, yeah? I saw you at The Sunday Show the other day. Yeah, you were funny, still!'

It gives you a real lift. When you're walking around where you grew up there are people, obviously, who have known you since you were a kid. They're invested in you doing well, so they will champion you at any given time. But, in saying that, there's not a roadmap that takes you from being unknown to getting a bit of fame. You have to make it all up as you go along – and then suddenly you might take a quantum leap that you just never expected or saw coming.

I can tell you exactly when that happened for me.

It happened when I made a Snapchat video about the different kind of MCs that you see at a rave, and I uploaded it to my Instagram. It was just a bit of fun, really. A pure piece of observational comedy and nostalgia I'd done at comedy nights before that had gone down well. I'd always had a knack for impersonating people, so I did a little bit about the types of MCs I remembered from growing up:

- The MC who misses the drop
- The MC who keeps repeating the same lyric
- The sound-effect-loving MC
- The off-beat MC
- The Jamaican MC

I can still remember the date I uploaded it: 17 December 2016. My girlfriend and I went to the cinema that evening, and as any guy knows, you can't have your phone out when you're with your girl. I had a quick peek before I put it on airplane mode and saw that my video was already getting more views than I normally got.

Rah! OK!

I checked my phone again when the movie was over, and it was up into the thousands.

The thing with social media is that when something goes viral, it never goes really viral on your own page. Someone else will put it on their bigger platform, and *then* it goes viral, which is what happened to me.

GRM Daily and Link Up TV put my video up. After that, the numbers started going up pretty quickly. I was becoming viral. As the views soared, it was a race against time for me to get them to tag my account and reroute people back to my profile. That was the crucial thing.

I saw the video was going viral, and when I logged on to Facebook twenty-four hours later, I saw that it had got a million views on the GRM Daily page. *Wow! A million people have watched me!*

Then I got famous people commenting on the video, like Stormzy, and Megaman from So Solid Crew. That felt proper mad to me; So Solid Crew were commenting on my little video. Man, the first two or three days after it went up were insane!

It was weird because the 'Types of MCs' video was something that I might, maybe, do live when performing stand-up, but I'd never normally make a video of it. I used to just mess about on Snapchat. But after I put the video up, loads more people started following me, and I saw my socials growing bigger and bigger.

After that, I did a second MCs video and it started off well. That one went viral as well, and then I started doing this thing where I would tease doing another one. I put up another post where I think I said, 'If I get a thousand likes for this, I'll drop a part three.'

Those thousand likes came ten minutes after I posted that message!

It was bizarre just to see how fast it was growing. I was buzzing about it, but I didn't necessarily want to be known for that alone. I was keen to carry on expanding my range and show more people what else I could do.

That is the one thing I always remember when I was first started doing those videos. I was practically gaining this audience overnight and beginning to think about how I could turn it into something. My socials grew and grew and grew to the point where, before I knew it, I'd hit 10,000 followers.

There were 10,000 people following me! *Me!* That's a lot to take in. It's half the capacity of The O2! Compared to today's standards that might not seem like that much, but I could see something was happening. It was exciting! But it was only the start. Within months, it went up to 50,000, then 70,000 ... and then, after about six months, I reached 100,000 followers. That is *a lot* of people! (Way more than you could fit in The O2!)

· · ·

I was uploading videos on Facebook, Twitter, Instagram and was posting about my stand-up comedy, but I never talked about it at work. What's mad, really, is that when I hit 10,000 followers, I was *still* working in retail. My colleagues still thought stand-up was a little hobby I had going on the side, like playing guitar at the weekend or something ('Oh, do you? That's nice!'). It wasn't that they wouldn't have supported me. I just didn't shout about it in my everyday life.

It was like I was leading a double life. By then I'd already been on CBBC and I'd been doing stand-up comedy for a good five years, but I didn't like inviting my work friends to any of my gigs and stuff. I just figured that doing comedy was one thing and working in retail was another. I kept them separate.

That's how it was. I didn't say anything. It wasn't insecurity or anything, I just didn't want all the attention on me in the shop because I was really only there to earn money and pay off my bills.

But one day, this customer in the shop came up to me and said, 'Oh my God, I saw your video! So funny, like!'

And everybody I worked with became a bit more curious after that.

I was a bit embarrassed at first but, looking back, this encounter in the shop was the first real moment of recognition for me. It was a personal landmark and moved me beyond hood fame. It's one thing to get the views, likes and followers online, but having people come up to you makes it real.

So, I kept on posting more videos – one of them went so big that I couldn't believe it.

In a way, I still can't.

It was just a simple thing: a video of two characters that I spontaneously came up with on a sunny day. I called the clip, 'When Cockney Guys See a Bit of Sun.'

I put a flat cap on and stood on the balcony of my mum's house (because I was still living with her at the time). I duct-taped my phone to a rickety tripod and started talking into the camera. I squinted and wiped my brow as if it were crazy hot and totally unbearable, and said:

'Fackin' 'ell, it's a bit hot! Jesus fackin' Christ, it's like Jamaica!' I said in my thickest geezer accent.

Then I called back into the room behind me, to my imaginary wife:

'Julie! Julie! Get a coupla cans in! Get a coupla cans, love!'

Then I segued into another character: a roadman, a.k.a a streetwise, would-be gangster. I put my puffa jacket on, stood by the window, and, while playing him, was pretending that the thirty-degree heat didn't bother him:

'Blud, why are people gassin' like it's hot an' that, bruv? I'm not even sweatin', bruv! It's just a little bit hot, you feel me?' I'd splashed my face and literally had water streaming from my temples.

Filming it was proper funny. My mum's back garden has a hedge at the end with a park on the other side. There is a hole in the hedge, and anyone walking past can see through it right up to her balcony.

While I was doing the sketch, if anybody strolled by and stared through the hedge, I stopped filming, ran inside the room and hid behind the curtain. It made shooting it a bit of a stop-start affair!

I did one take that was going really smoothly. It was flowing and I was getting properly into it, then I saw a guy walk past the hedge, stare through the gap and do a double take. Fifteen seconds later, he walked back the other way and peered through again. I could see that he was thinking:

What's that bloke doing on his balcony, in a flat cap, waving a can about and talking to himself? What a weirdo!

I could see his point! But it was worth it. I uploaded the video to Instagram and that afternoon it went absolutely crazy. I was getting thousands of likes and shares. I couldn't keep up – they were racking up every second! And it made me realise:

Woah! People really like these characters!

And then … Drake followed me on Instagram.

What?

The thing with Drake is that he's always had his finger on the pulse of what is going on in UK culture and music. Even so, I still have no idea what brought him to my Instagram videos. I'd love to ask him one day!

I didn't even know it had happened till I started getting calls and texts telling me, 'Shit, Mo, Drake is following you!' *Huh? Is he?* I checked, and there he was. It was great but it all felt proper mad. I did a post about it on Twitter:

Mo Gilligan

Got a follow from Drake on Instagram but my mum still hasn't accepted my friend request on Facebook 😂 nah using her good face creams today

---

It was a mad time. I was still folding jeans but at the same time I was going more and more viral and watching my followers rocket through the roof.

I could tell from the reaction and the comments on my socials that people especially loved the geezer character – I think I had struck a chord with that one! Everyone knows a geezer, right?

So, I put a new geezer video up – and this is the one that still does the rounds today. The character was back on the balcony, in his flat cap, still grinning and squinting in the sunshine, still talking to his woman, who was telling him that she'd got him a present:

'What, you got me a present?' he said. 'You treatin' me, you slag?'

The next second, he was wearing a string vest.

'Fackin' 'ell, Julie, this is nice!' he said. 'I like it! It's breathable! What's it called?'

'A string vest,' says Julie.

'A string vest? A vest, made out of string? Who thought of it? I feel like a yardie!'

Then I did another one where the geezer was singing a bit of a song. I posted one where he said, 'It's like Barbados!' – Drake replied to that one on Instagram with a Barbadian flag!

My mum was at work one day when one of her colleagues pulled the video up on his phone. 'Have you seen this "Coupla Cans" guy?' he asked her. 'It's hilarious!'

'That's my son!' Mum said, proudly.

The views and the likes kept on going up and up. It was great and it had a massive upside ... but also a downside.

Before going viral, I never anticipated what recognition and fame would be like. My perception of fame was still what I had grown up with – the wax figures and memorabilia at Planet Hollywood. The stars always seemed so distant in those days.

Modern fame is different.

It's a double-edged sword. It leads to better things, sure, but the more success you get, the more intrusive it is on your personal life. Celebrities nowadays are closer to their fans than ever before. And it leaves you more exposed.

When a post starts going viral, you have people messaging you:

'Hey man, really funny video!'

Other people start sharing it. You're reading all the comments under it as well, because you can't help yourself.

Some people are like, '*Rah*, this is funny!'

But then other commenters will say stuff like this:

'This is dead, bruv! It's not even funny. This is shit! *I* could've done this. Is this what comedy is nowadays?'

So, I had to start dealing with online trolls and other negative stuff. And at the same time, I felt indebted to the people who did like my videos, like I owed them a piece of myself. Once I started to gain a large following, that feeling would be in the back of my mind whenever I uploaded something.

Alongside the videos, I was still doing gigs and I saw my social media presence definitely having an effect on those shows. It was raising my profile. I still wasn't headlining too many shows, but I was definitely moving up the bill and, for the first time ever, I'd hear that audience members were excited to see *me*.

People started saying, 'Oh, I know that guy! I've seen his clips online! Yeah, I'll pay to go see him!'

I liked that a lot. It meant I was working my way up the under-card, like a boxer, doing longer sets (and being paid a bit more) but without the pressure of being the headliner who had to carry the show. It was almost like the benefits without the pressure.

I was getting offered more things off the back of the clips, like going on Radio 1Xtra, and it was also pulling more people into Cracking Up Comedy. Now I'd put the tickets up on sale, and *boom!* They were gone in five minutes. There would always be queues stretching down the street outside the Ace Miranda, and we'd even have to start turning people away. *Wicked!*

• • •

While all of this was going on, I was also planning to go to The Fringe. I knew that I had fucked up the previous year, with my rubbish audition in Nottingham, but this year I was determined to get there, by one means or another

The thing is that Edinburgh, to me, felt like a rite of passage for comedians. I figured if I could tick it off the list, it would be another accomplishment that solidified all of the work I'd been putting in. I even had a name for my show: *Momentum*.

It's not easy to get your foot in the door at The Fringe. It costs up to ten grand to go there and put on a show. You've gotta pay for your venue, PR, accommodation and all of the other stuff. The stakes are pretty high in the sense that you can easily spend all of that money and not even get a return. It's a big risk.

For all the recognition I was getting, I still didn't know how I was going to find the money to get to Edinburgh anyway. Making viral videos doesn't pay the bills.

At the same time, with my socials, I was starting to get business enquiries in my DMs, like:

Hi, Mo! We can give you £100 if you can post this video about our teeth-whitening product.

But I was always adamant I wasn't just gonna sell out like that. I didn't want to have painstakingly built up this social media platform, then suddenly mislead people by telling them to buy teeth-whitening products.

There was one time when I was doing a gig in Amsterdam and had agreed to put the sponsor's logo on my video. But that felt different because it didn't change the content of my videos. I was basically just selling advertising space.

I've always felt like I have an organic online following. People like what I post, and back then I was always trying to push what I could do in terms of videos. I didn't want to spoil that.

In any case, I had an even bigger problem than the money when it came to going to Edinburgh. I was still doing shop work, by now in Levi's, and at that point I had pushed it to the limit in terms of how much time I could take off.

I only had two weeks' leave available for the whole year, but now I had to ask them if I could go away for the entire month of August. But my manager said, 'Ah, I don't know if that's going to be possible because we need you here. We have the summer sale.'

It was shaping up to be a bit of a problem.

So, I had this big conundrum: *I need to find ten grand to go to Edinburgh, and I also need to get the time off!*

I met with a promoter who was heading up to The Fringe. He wasn't one of the big-name ones, but he seemed good, and he said that he was willing to put on my show.

Woah! This made me feel as if I was on my way! Getting a promoter is a big step! But it wasn't that straightforward.

It's important to get a promoter because they basically put your show onstage and get bums in seats. Sometimes the promoters will foot the bill upfront to put on a show and only recoup their costs later. Whatever profits you make in ticket sales, you might be able to keep, but often performers only ever break even. Or worse, if your show doesn't sell well you might end up in debt and have to do shows later in the year to pay off the promoter.

This guy wouldn't do it like that. He wanted an advance. He was telling me, 'I need three grand by the end of the month'. *Shit!* I was thinking, *Three grand? How am I going to get three grand in the next couple of weeks?*

In my head, I was trying to work out all sorts of plans:

I can do a lot more overtime at work. I can maybe raise a grand. But where is the rest going to come from?

I knew I had to start thinking outside of the box and did a small show with some friends of mine. They were putting on a music show at the Ritzy in Brixton, so I said, 'Look, I'll host it, we can do a collab and we'll split the profits fifty-fifty.'

It was great. It sold out so quickly because people were coming to see 'that guy from the videos' they watched online, and I earned a little money that could go towards my Edinburgh fund. I had to try stuff like that because I don't have friends or family members that can just drop me two grand.

I was trying to make all sorts of plans. I was thinking, *Maybe I can take out a loan from the bank, and just pay it off within a year's time if I get a good interest rate?* I went back to the promoter and said I'd raise the money but I needed a little more time.

At first, I said to him, 'Can you give me six weeks?'

'No.'

'A month?'

'No. I need it by next week.'

What? It felt like a big setback. It was frustrating. I thought to myself, *Who's getting you three grand in seven days? What do you think this is?*

So, I decided that I couldn't go to Edinburgh.

I felt like I was in limbo. My socials were really starting to go up, but I was still working in retail. I knew that if I wanted to pursue my dreams, I needed to leave this safety net and take the opportunities that were starting to come in.

In the end, I didn't think too long and hard about it. I had always known there'd be a time that I'd have to leave retail for good, and I guess I had been mentally preparing for that moment. By now, I was getting offered all sorts of decent opportunities, like the trial spot on 1Xtra.

Not many of them were paid jobs, but they were things that I had never been offered before. That's when I decided that it was time to take the leap.

It started off with me messaging the assistant manager to try to get a shift swapped. I would get my shifts sent over in fortnightly rotas; I was always having to try to swap shifts to fit around my actual passion: comedy.

This particular day, I asked the manager, yet again, 'Can I swap my shift and do another day instead?' But this time she was like, 'No, unfortunately you can't, Mo, because we need you to close up the shop and nobody else can do it that day.'

I listened to her, and suddenly there was an angel and devil on my shoulder, talking to me, and both of them were saying, *'This is the time! Leave!'*

'OK,' I wrote back. 'If that's the case, I think I'm just going to have to leave. It's been lovely working here but it's not going to work with timetables and stuff. I don't want to be a person that just doesn't come into work and lets everyone down, so I think I'd rather just leave.'

'Alright, that's no problem,' she said. 'That's fine.'

And that was the end of my career in retail. It was surprisingly easy, but in the back of my mind I was still nervous that it might not work out.

•   •   •

And then in May 2017, just one month after I left, I got an email. I remember I was sitting on the stairs at home when I read it. It said:

Hi Mo,

This is BET International. We'd love to take you to LA for the BET Awards. If you put some content on your socials for us, we'll pay for your flight and accommodation.

I read this email – and I suddenly realised that my hand was shaking.

They're going to take me to LA?!

I'd never been to America before. Three weeks earlier I'd been trying to swap shifts, selling shirts, and wasn't able to go to The Fringe … and now one of the biggest American networks, Black Entertainment Television, wanted to take me to their big annual awards show?

I read it again and again. I swear to you – I just couldn't believe it.

My fortunes had changed so much in such a small amount of time. Instead of begging the shop manager for time off to go to Edinburgh, I'd been invited to a huge event in America. And I didn't even have to ask if I could swap my shifts no more!

So, I flew to LA.

BET flew a few people out, like Lateysha Grace off MTV and another comedian, Don't Jealous Me.

The three of us got picked up from the hotel in LA in a big blacked-out SUV for the BET Awards at the Staples Theater in downtown LA. When we got there, there was a whole convoy of cars waiting to drop people off. Security men were opening the car doors to let the stars out. There were fans lined up, screaming as actors and rappers climbed out of their cars. They even started screaming at us, even though they had no clue who we were.

'Woooooooh! Yeaaaaaah!'

I had never even been to an award show in London before and now here I was, at a mad, big show in Hollywood! I got out the car, looked all round me and took a deep breath.

Whew, this is A BIG DEAL, man! This is no joke!

And then we realised … we had forgotten our tickets to get in.

We felt so *stupid*! We had left our tickets in the hotel. We were with somebody from BET, so we were thinking maybe it would be OK and we could talk our way in, but that didn't work, so Don't Jealous Me had to race back to the hotel to get our tickets.

While I was waiting for him to come back, I was watching the red carpet. The awards had a proper red carpet outside the Microsoft Theater. There were loads of paparazzi there – it was literally like how you see it in the movies and on TV.

They were waiting for the big stars. Some of the celebs hung around on the red carpet and some of them just rushed through. Everyone was waiting for Cardi B and when she got there, she was ushered through by her entourage and security team pretty quick. But she stopped for a few photos – *FLASH! FLASH! FLASH!* – because that is one of the most important bits.

Then Don't Jealous Me got back with our tickets and it was our turn to go down the red carpet. I liked how Don't Jealous Me was proper on it. He didn't just skulk along the carpet – he was strutting like he belonged there: 'I don't know about you but I'm getting my picture taken, bruv!'

I didn't even know if I should walk down the red carpet. Like, nobody in Hollywood, or in America, was going to know who Mo the Comedian was! I was feeling a bit shy: *What's the fucking point?* But Don't Jealous Me was so into it that I just followed his lead.

We walked onto the red carpet and it was just like a cattle farm. We weren't going to be ushered through like Cardi B. Everyone was trying to get on the carpet. People were pushing and treading on the long dresses and whatnot: *Hey, dude! Watch out!*

Then we got to a woman with a clipboard who was talking to everyone as they reached her. She looked me up and down.

'Hi there! What's your name?' she asked.

'Mo Gilligan.'

'OK, Mo! What do you do?'

And I realised that this was the woman who decided if you get to walk down the main red carpet past the paparazzi into the venue. Because if you were a nobody, you got sent around the back way, away from all of the photographers.

So, I told her: 'Yeah, I'm a footballer! I play in the Premier League back home in the UK!'

She smiled. She liked that answer.

'Oh, OK, great!' she said. And she called over to the photographers, 'This is Mo Gilligan, a British professional footballer. Premier League!'

There was a spot marked out on the carpet for the celebs to stand on, and I walked out onto it. The cameras started whirring. I was blinded by the lights and all I could hear were voices shouting at me:

'Over here, man!'

Flash! Flash! Flash! Flash!

'Look this way, dude!'

Flash! Flash! Flash! Flash!

'Mo, Mo! Look to me!'

Flash! Flash! Flash! Flash!

They were taking loads of pictures! All I could see was a sea of cameras flashing. *Flash flash flash!*

I was so gassed! I felt like Will Smith. All the US press were there, and TV programmes like *Good Morning America*. It was totally amazing …

Except that, let me tell you, I've never seen even one of those pictures. Not one! I went on Getty Images the next day and I was searching high and low. Nope. Nothing. I never made it onto Getty Images.

I was fuming. I thought, *A picture will look great on my socials! Mo at the BET Awards!* But I never found one. It's almost like they found out that there's not really a Premier League footballer named Mo Gilligan ...

Once we got into the awards ceremony itself, it was unbelievable. I realised: *This isn't just hood fame now! It's not being recognised by a customer while you're selling jeans!* I sat in the theatre, three rows in, and looked around me.

Busta Rhymes is two seats from me! Floyd Mayweather Jr is over there!

I couldn't believe the people I was sitting with, and the people I was watching perform. Bruno Mars opened up the show. I saw Migos perform, and Mary J. Blige, and A$AP Rocky. Solange Knowles was presenting an award, and Cardi B, and Jamie Foxx, and Lil' Kim.

At times I had to pinch myself! *Am I really here? I'm a young Black boy from south London and I'm seeing fame on this level.* Stars in America are so idolized – they're practically treated like gods. Everything that night felt bigger, more amplified, and I gazed around with one thought in my head:

This is fucking nuts!

But it was a great night. From working in retail three weeks ago to now, where I was having pictures taken on a red carpet in

Hollywood – *of me!* But it was also a lesson in patience, taking a risk and making that leap in your career.

Like I said, there is no roadmap for success.

Things happen that are outside of your control. But I've always found that real growth comes in those moments when you've got to make a difficult decision. And, you know what? If you go from folding jeans to sitting in Hollywood watching Migos, two seats away from Busta Rhymes, you can't be doing too bad ...

10

THAT MOMENT WHEN ...

You Find People Will Pay To See You

*M*y trip to LA was amazing, but when I got back, it felt like time to do some serious planning and work out exactly what I was doing and where I was going. I suppose it felt like a real make-or-break time back then.

I met up with Polly and Geli at their house and we sat down, took stock and assessed exactly where I was up to:

- I was no longer folding shirts (good)
- I was playing shows all over the country and putting on Cracking Up Comedy (good)
- My social media following was exploding and the numbers were getting bigger and bigger (good)
- I was still skint most of the time (bad)
- I wasn't going to the Edinburgh Festival (bad)

By the end of the meeting, we had agreed on the ideal next step for me. It was something I had wanted for a long time but had hardly dared to dream of.

It was time for me to try to go on tour.

I knew in my heart it was what I wanted to do. A headline tour, under my own name – every comic's dream! I suppose the big question was if I was ready to do it.

I knew that I *felt* ready. By now, I'd done The Sunday Show, I'd done Black comedy shows, mainstream shows, a tiny bit of TV and was being followed by thousands of people on socials – but would those people who watched me for free on their screens take a gamble and pay to see me play live?

Well, there was only one way to find out.

Initially, I thought I might try to organise the tour myself and sell tickets online, like I did with Cracking Up Comedy. But when I came to look at it, the structure for doing a national tour like that just wasn't in place. Doing it through a small ticket website just wasn't going to work.

No, I needed a *proper*, big, tour promoter. So, we went to the biggest one in the world.

Polly fixed us up a meeting with Live Nation, the giant tour-promotions company. Not just that: we were meeting Ian Coburn, their head of comedy who had booked massive tours and nights at The O2 for people like Dave Chappelle, Kevin Hart and Micky Flanagan.

Woah! We're in the big league!

Some people say you should always go to meetings like that in a suit but on the day, I decided just to *be me*. It was a hot day, so I got on the Tube in a T-shirt, shorts and white trainers, and got off the Bakerloo line at Oxford Circus. I was ten minutes late to meet Polly at Live Nation (sadly, this is pretty normal for me!).

Polly, Ian and I sat in their huge boardroom, and Ian asked me, 'OK, what is it that you want to do?' And I told him that I wanted to do a comedy tour.

'Hmm,' he said. 'We love what you do, Mo, but we've tried doing tours with social media stars and YouTubers, and it can be difficult ...'

I was honest with him. 'I hear what you're saying,' I said. 'But I'm a comedian first and foremost. That's what I do. I've been playing live shows for years and I think a tour is the next step ...'

It worked and Ian jumped on board, so we came up with a plan. I said that I'd like to try to do dates in Manchester, Birmingham and Bristol, but I knew London was the place I *might* do pretty well. And I wanted to pursue a particular strategy in the capital.

I suggested that rather than try to hit big venues, we should do smaller shows in north, south, east and west London. I didn't know if people would trek right across town to see me, but I did think they might come out if I was local to them.

We all agreed on the plan, and we decided there and then that we would call it *The Coupla Cans Tour*. Because that phrase, that video, was what I was best known for at that point.

OK. Here we go!

We left the meeting and I went straight across the road to the Apple store. Kae Kurd, another comic and a friend of mine, was working there part-time. I sought him out, among the customers gawping at iPads and MacBooks, and I told him:

'Dude, Live Nation want to do my tour and, if you're up for it, I'd like you to be my support!'

'That sounds great!' he said. 'I'll just have to talk to my bosses about getting time off ...'

A while earlier, I had asked a photographer mate, Amir Shah, to take some stock photos for me. He was like, 'Sure, Mo!' But the day we came to do them, I had on a T-shirt that I noticed had loads of bits of fluff stuck to it.

Tssch! I can't do photos with these bits of fluff stuck to me!

Amir let me put his T-shirt on instead. It was quite a thick shirt and had a hood on it. And then we started taking photos that I could use to promote my comedy shows.

There is a weird thing about the posters for comedy shows. The comedian has to always look confused and kind of surprised: 'Huh? What? I'm doing a comedy show? Me?' It seems like it's some kind of official comedy law – the posters outside the venue have to be *wacky*.

I've never been that keen on that, but we went ahead and did a few like that anyway. And what image did we end up using for *The Coupla Cans Tour*? Me, in somebody else's thick hooded T-shirt with no fluff on it, looking confused, surprised and wacky.

The tour was kicking off in October 2017 and the tickets went on sale in July. Of course, I was hammering my socials, telling my followers all about it. And when the tickets went on sale, I wanted to see how easy the buying experience was.

As soon as the tickets went on sale at ten o'clock, I went to the Live Nation website and clicked to try to buy tickets for one of my London shows. *Nothing happened.* It seemed like it was jammed. I just got an error message: 'Tickets are unavailable. Please refresh page.'

Ah, shit, man! I didn't want *this*! My tickets going on sale, and there's a fault on the site and people can't buy them! I had a look at my socials, and there were people complaining about the same thing: 'I'm trying to buy them, but the site's not working!'

I clicked on the other dates, like Manchester, which seemed to be OK, but I couldn't get anywhere with the London shows. I tried buying one single ticket, because there are always singles floating around, but even that wasn't working. I was getting proper vexed about it.

Damn! We need to tell Live Nation about this problem …

And then Polly called me.

'*Oh. My. God. Mo!*' she said. 'Oh my God!'

'What is it?'

'They've sold out!' she told me. 'Live Nation have just told me that all of your London dates sold out in two minutes.'

What?

I could not believe my ears. '*This is mad, Polly!*'

'Yeah!' she said. She was laughing, the same as I was. 'They want to put some more London shows up, straight away!'

They did, and … they sold out as well. It became a theme. Every time we added a new London show, it sold out in minutes. It was unbelievable. People thought it couldn't be true and that I was hoaxing them.

'Nah, Mo, man!' they were telling me. 'You're pretending – your tickets aren't selling out this quick, though!'

'They are!' I'd say. 'I'm not making it up!'

The other gigs were going OK, as well. We had a date in Cambridge that sold out, and then Manchester did the same. The show in Birmingham was at a big venue that held about a thousand people. When *that* one sold out, I knew we were in business.

In a weird way, it felt a bit like watching TV on general election night, when they might say, 'Oh, and Labour have taken Cambridge!' I was watching shows sell out, and it felt like 'Yes! We've got Manchester!' And then I had friends telling me:

'Mo, man, we tried to get tickets for your London shows but they're all gone! So, we're going to drive up to Cambridge ...'

It was amazing! Ticket sales were going beyond my wildest imagination. I should really have felt on top of the world ... and yet, somehow, I didn't.

• • •

In the four months or so before my tour started, I had absolutely no money. I had left my job, so I didn't have that source of regular income anymore, and I had no other real way of earning. It was a hard time.

I carried on doing Cracking Up Comedy, because I needed it to make a bit of money, and Live Nation were still telling me that tour sales were going well. But I had no money in my pocket and my credit-card debt was spiralling. It was one of the toughest times of my life.

I was in a weird limbo still: neither one thing nor the other. My videos going viral meant that my fame was spreading beyond just hood fame. More and more people seemed to know who I was. I would be walking down the street and people driving their cars would shout out the window.

'Hey, Mo! Can I get a little selfie?' People used to jump out their cars in the middle of traffic.

'Yeah, cool!'

'Ah, I love the geezer man! Come on, do it for me! Do the voice!'

So, I'd do it. Or I'd be on the Tube, or a bus, and somebody would come running over: 'Mo! Can I have a picture?'

'Yeah.'

'Great! And another one? Do the roadman for us!'

I'd always say yes. Anyone who wanted a video, I'd do one for them. I felt obligated to do it, because I knew that it was because of my followers that I was kind of getting somewhere. But it felt a bit weird after a while.

I went to Wireless Festival in Finsbury Park but could hardly move for people putting a phone in my face. At one point there was a queue of people lining up for pictures. Everyone seemed to know who I was – and yet I was worried about going to the bar and buying myself a drink in case my card was declined.

It was such a bizarre time. Brands started giving me free stuff. Adidas gave me a lot of clothes. Beats by Dre sent me a pair of headphones. Tinie Tempah invited me to the launch of his Smart car with Disturbing London. It was all cool … but I kind of felt like I still hadn't really achieved anything yet.

I felt like I was a passenger on somebody else's journey. It was all out of my control. And I was still in debt, without a penny to my name. All I could do was wait for my tour to start so I could take that next big leap.

•   •   •

That August bank holiday, I got invited to a daytime rave. I was going to meet a load of my friends there. Only this rave had a very particular theme. It was an all-white party.

I had white jeans and white creps on but didn't have a fresh white shirt, so I made a plan. I knew there was a clothes shop right around the corner from the party, so I decided to go there in my normal clothes. I would buy a shirt and change into my party outfit in the changing room.

So, that was what I did. And then I was walking through the middle of London, dirty old London, on a bright sunny bank holiday, in a white shirt, white jeans and white trainers. I looked like an angel but felt like an absolute dork, or an extended member of Blazin' Squad.

When I got to the party, my mates were already in the club so I had to wait in a long line on my own. I saw a few people in the queue looking at me and nudging each other, which made me feel even more self-conscious.

When I finally got inside, it was crazy hot in the club. It took me a while to find my friends, and when I did, I couldn't even afford to buy a drink. I was stuck in a sweat pit, dressed like an angel, but in a venue that was hot as hell. It felt like the Central line in the middle of a heatwave. I started complaining to my mates, telling them I wanted to go home.

Just as I was contemplating leaving, one of my friends held out his phone. 'Look at this!' he said.

I had a quick look. Drake had put a picture on his Instagram. It was him and Giggs, the rapper, hanging out at Reading Festival. Drake was about to join Giggs onstage, as his special guest.

'Cool,' I said. 'Drake came out last minute?'

'No, Mo, look at the caption!' he said to me. And I read it.

Below the picture, Drake had written:

> **champgnepapi** ✔ Enjoying this 'Julie bring me a couple cans' weather today.

Oh. My. Gosh! That's my slogan! And Drake has just used it on his Instagram!

I lost my mind! I was just like, *Wow!* I didn't know what to do. I went upstairs in the club to get better phone reception but I'd already missed four calls. There were voicemails, and they were all saying the same thing:

'Shit, Mo, have you seen this? Drake has just shouted you out on Instagram!'

I phoned my mum:

'Mum, Drake has said "Coupla Cans" on Instagram!'

'Has he?' she asked. 'That's nice for him.'

Mum really didn't get the importance of what had just happened! Well, it wasn't her fault – I mean, why should she? But my head was in a whirl.

There was one person that I knew *would* get it. Michael Dapaah was at the same stage in his comedy career as me. He was doing sketches that were going viral and had just started doing his Big Shaq character on YouTube. I would bump into him at events, and launches, and it was all as new for him as it was for me. He was the only person who understood the magnitude of what I was going through at that time.

I called Michael but I didn't even need to say anything. 'Ah, bruv, I've just seen it, man!' he said, as soon as he picked up. 'That's so sick!'

After that, I went back into the main party. I felt re-energised, totally lifted up, and everyone was coming up to me, one by one.

'Mo, man! Have you seen this thing on Drake's Instagram ...'

'Yeah ...'

'Bruv, that is wicked! Can I get you a drink?'

I was happy to accept the drinks, because I couldn't afford to get one myself!

For the next two or three days, the story was everywhere. All of the channels that would usually share my stuff, like GRM Daily and Link Up TV, were talking about it, and I was sharing them. I even gained some American followers who started leaving nice comments on my posts.

Drake's shout-out could not have been better timed. My tickets for the tour had been going great anyway, but now they started flying out at double-speed, not just in London, but *everywhere*. Live Nation started adding more dates. It seemed that a lot of people were thinking:

If Drake's backing Mo, I'm gonna back him!

It put me on so many more people's radar. It's too simplistic to say that Drake's backing *made* me. But it was certainly a pivotal point in my career.

• • •

By the time I came to start *The Coupla Cans Tour*, the whole run had sold out. Every extra date that we had added had sold out. And I just knew, more than anything, that the tour had to be special because I realised that a lot of people coming to see me might not have been to a comedy show before. And I figured that it was my duty to make it a night that they would never forget.

The first night of the tour, 1 October 2017, was in Cardiff, which meant a lot to me because I still had a lot of family there. All of those childhood memories of school holidays in south Wales and waiting for money from my granddad came flooding back to me.

But also, on that first night, I realised: *I don't know who is coming to this tour. It's sold out – but what kind of audience is it?*

Was it all going to be young people? Older people? Black? White? I hadn't been on a panel show or been able to do much to promote the tour, which meant the only places to hear about it had been Live Nation and my socials. I was interested to see what my fans looked like.

There was a long curtain along the front of the stage but before the show, as the auditorium was filling up, I peeked through it. I could see groups of girls, and groups of guys. There was an older White couple sitting right at the front, and that razzed me:

Rah! THOSE guys know who I am!

As I was peeping out, a couple of girls in the audience spotted me and squealed out: 'Look, there's Mo! You alright, Mo?' I shut the curtains quick, and scarpered back to my dressing room.

Was I nervous? I was, for probably all of thirty seconds ... but all of those years of paying my dues, up and down the country, paid off. I went straight into show mode.

I came out at the start of the show as my geezer character, with a couple of cans in a bag, which got a huge cheer from the audience. I said a few words then introduced Kae Kurd. After Kae, I came back out as the roadman character and then, after the interval, I did the rest of the set as myself. Mo Gilligan had arrived.

It went great. It went really, really great. I felt like all the jokes were hitting and people were bussin' up and completely into it. I couldn't have hoped for a better start ... and then we went into full-on tour mode.

Touring is such a weird experience. You just fall into this strange way of living, this weird day-to-day routine, that unfolds by its own logic: *Go to the hotel. Unpack. Go to the venue. Do a mic check. Get all your clothes and stuff out. Prepare. Perform the show. Grab something to eat. Sleep. Wake up. Pack. Repeat ...*

It was the first time I'd lived such a full-on lifestyle, but I soon got used to it.

Every show seemed to go better than the last ... and I was finding it very interesting to check out my audiences and interact with them. You can always tell the people who aren't used to going to comedy gigs and don't know how they work. They are the ones who will be up at the bar while you are on, getting drinks for all their friends. They are having a great time: '*Rah! This is comedy!*'

And then you speak to them from the stage, and they freeze.

'Hey, how are you doing? Wassup?'

'What? Me?'

'Yeah, you! What's your name?'

'Er … I don't know!'

Then you get the other people in the crowd, who think they can heckle the comic. I got a few of those on *The Coupla Cans Tour*. There is just one thing that hecklers always forget: *the comic has got the mic.*

If a heckler starts on a comedian, there is nothing to stop the comic from hitting back and making his entire show about that guy. Roasting him for the whole night. I've done it before, and it's not really nice, but sometimes the heckler just leaves you no choice.

It's kind of brutal, and it sort of goes back to medieval times. Imagine a king is speaking to a crowd of royal subjects. If one of those subjects wants to start an uprising and shouts out, 'Come on, we can get 'im!', then the others might think they can depose the king.

It's down to the king to stop them. And if the king tells his guards, 'Who was that? Get that guy and chop off his head!' then the citizens are gonna quickly change their tune. They're gonna be like:

'Shit, this king is chopping off heads! Nah, I'm not involved, man! I'm just here, all quiet, making my bread and stirring my cheese …'

It's a bit like that with comedy. Now, I'm not a comic who likes to make the show all about people in the audience, because I've got material to use. (Also, I'm not a king.) But at the same time, if people think they can say negative stuff to me onstage, I have to bring back the kid from the playground who'd roast his friends with yo mama jokes.

I do like to talk to the people in the first two rows at my shows. So, I might ask a guy:

'Hey, wassup, dude? Are you out on a date tonight?'

The guy might think he's a bad man. He might frown at me, and say:

'Why you asking, bruv?'

Then I'm like, 'Woah, woah, ooo-kaaay! Someone's angry! I think I might talk to somebody else instead!'

Everyone starts laughing – and, if I'm lucky, the guy that I'm talking to might change from the Incredible Hulk to Bruce Banner. I never want to get at people in the audience and go after them. But, if they put me in that position, I will.

I remember years ago that I did one little show, which I was going out after from, so I wasn't really dressed like a comic. I had tight cropped trousers on, so you could see my ankles. I made a joke about it: 'Guys, I know you can see my ankles today! I apologise that they're a bit dry!'

Everyone started laughing, but then, as I started my set, this guy in the crowd shouted out:

'Yeah, and your hair looks shit as well!'

What? I looked out into the audience to try to see where the guy was and spotted him. After that, I spoke to the show technician.

'Can we just have the lights up, please?'

The guy turned the lights on, and every head turned towards the geezer who had heckled me about my hair … who was sitting there with a big old quiff. Man, it was such an open goal!

'And you think *my* hair looks stupid?' I asked him. 'Are you not going to address the fact that you have an Elvis quiff? And we're not in 1958?'

The audience was bussin' up laughing and I ended up making nearly all of the show about this guy. I didn't like doing it but I had to let him know that he couldn't just turn up and try to wreck my set. I ain't a king but when I'm onstage, I'm trying to have a good time and just want everyone to enjoy themselves as much as I do – even the Elvis impersonator.

•   •   •

A lot of things I had picked up in my years of playing shows, and putting on Cracking Up Comedy, came together on *The Coupla Cans Tour*. It all fell into place. And one of the most crucial things was the importance of being *relatable*.

I think I had picked up on that when I first saw Slim in Deptford. He had – and still does – this persona that makes you really like him. In a weird way, you felt like you knew him even before he started to perform. Even before he'd told a single joke. He makes you feel like he's your mate, and that is such a cool skill to have. Not many comics have that knack when it comes to delivering their material to an audience. Being relatable is, in some ways, even better than having the best material.

When I was starting out, I used to focus so hard on trying to be the best comic on the bill, the funniest man in the room. But I've learnt now that that's not necessarily the way to go. If you're relatable, it gets people on your side from the start.

I often compare it to football.

Yes, there are the top players who have the best skills and the record-breaking stats. But as a kid the player I most loved to watch was Ronaldinho – because he made football look effortless and so much fun. *Woah, man! You're having a great time doing that!*

I want people to have a great time watching me because they can see that I love what I'm doing. Because I do.

Anyway. *The Coupla Cans Tour* started off great. For the first week or two, it almost felt too good to be true.

But, despite how well it was all going, I wasn't in a great place, mentally. The adrenaline rush that came with performing every night felt like it filled the void.

• • •

About a month into the tour, I got invited to go on *The Russell Howard Hour* on Sky. I was gassed about that because a lot of comics I knew had been on and I was keen to do it.

I wanted to do a routine making up Rastafarian nursery rhymes, and I needed some music for it. I stayed up with my friend

Louis all of the night before writing music. We were working on it till six in the morning!

After about three hours' sleep, I got picked up in a big flashy Mercedes with blacked-out windows and was taken to the TV studio. That was sick but when I got there, I was put onstage with just the cameramen and technicians there, to rehearse, which felt weird. It's always odd doing comedy without an audience.

I was asking them about all the different cameras and when I had to look in which one. I had to learn on my feet, quickly!

The show itself went well, though. I was only on for five minutes. I started off doing a routine I have about how mums treat you when you're a kid, and I got some good laughs. Then the technician played my track and I went into the Rasta nursery rhymes:

'*Jack-and-Jill, go uppa da hill, yeah! To fetch a bucket of some water! He feed his daughter, he feed his daughter! Aye! Because she thirsty …*'

'*Three blind mice! Three blind mice! Them a look for the cheese but they can't find a slice! No cheese feed dem, feed dem! Because they lactose-intolerant …*'

'*Ol' MacDonald, 'im have a farm! [Beat] It is a … ganja farm!*'

People were bussin' up, but my slot was over pretty quick. I thought it had gone well in my head, but I was dying to see how it looked on TV. The frustrating thing was, we didn't have Sky so I couldn't even see it when it went out! I had to wait till someone stuck it on YouTube the next day.

When I did see it, I was relieved and pleased. I thought it looked OK. It had been my first ever stand-up on TV, and it made me feel like I was still making progress. *Moving forwards.*

•   •   •

About halfway through the tour, I was given the opportunity to extend the run and add some dates at Leicester Square Theatre in Soho.

'Hmm,' I said. 'I guess so. Maybe.'

Ian from Live Nation said there were twelve dates going there. *Twelve!* This sounded like far too many for me. We'd already played some London dates and had more lined up, so I didn't want to rinse people out with this tour.

'Nah, I feel like everyone who wants to see it will have bought tickets already,' I said.

'Trust me, you can add more dates,' Ian replied. 'But it's totally up to you. Your call. Do you want to do it?'

I thought, then took a deep breath. 'All right, cool! Fuck it! Let's do it!'

The Leicester Square tickets went on sale the next week. Usually, tickets go out on a Friday morning or a Saturday but we released them on a Sunday, which is weird. And that Sunday, we were on the way to Leeds for that night's show when I got the news that I'd sold out nine of the twelve dates already, and the other three were very close to selling out too.

Wow!

I think, in a funny way, getting that news was the moment when I actually realised: *You know what? This might just work! This*

might be my career … my life! I might just become a professional come-
dian, after all …

Leicester Square Theatre is an intimate, four-hundred-person theatre, about the same size that The Sunday Show had been, but we kept banging out night after night there. We ended up doing twenty-five shows all in all. I realised that some of the people who had already been to see *The Coupla Cans Tour* were coming back for more.

I knew that I had a lot of fans, through the online videos, who were under eighteen and I wanted to do shows that they could come to. We added a couple of matinees at the Leicester Square Theatre. It was a nice idea … but it didn't quite work out.

At the first matinee, I said, 'OK, who is under eighteen here?' And just three people put their hands up, out of a crowd of four hundred! It was exactly the same at the second one. They were just a normal audience who liked the afternoon show because it left them free to do something else in the evening.

A few of the Leicester Square shows were like out-of-body experiences. I'd be performing, but by now I knew the set and my stage directions so well that I'd be thinking about something else while I was doing it. That felt weird to me … but a lot of other performers have told me that they've had the same thing when they're onstage.

After each show, I'd go out and take photos with the audience. It wasn't a paid-for, VIP thing: I'd just tell them, 'Give me five minutes to rub my face down and I'll come out and do some pictures with you!' These people were there to see me, they'd spent money to watch me – I figured it was the least I could do.

I did loads and loads of selfies (and videos). We had to limit the video side of things a bit, because there were so many people and we wanted to give everyone a chance to get a picture.

Just as the Leicester Square dates were finally coming to an end, Ian at Live Nation got back in touch again.

'There's a two-week run going at the Vaudeville Theatre on The Strand in October,' he told me. 'Would you like to do it?'

Woah! This was something else! Leicester Square Theatre was cool, but the Vaudeville was a proper big, full-on West End theatre! And Ian and I had the same conversation again as before Leicester Square. I said I thought the tour was rinsed out but Ian said we could definitely do it.

'Yeah, go on then!' I told him. 'Let's try it!'

• • •

That summer, as I waited for the Vaudeville Theatre dates to come around, I went to Wireless Festival in Finsbury Park again.

It was great – Stormzy was on, and Migos, and Cardi B, and Giggs. DJ Khaled was supposed to headline the last night, on the Sunday, but he had to pull out very late, because he had some kind of travel issue or other.

But there were rumours going around that the Wireless promoters had pulled a rabbit out of the hat and got a great last-minute replacement headliner: Drake.

Woah! Could this be true?

On that Sunday, I was mostly chilling backstage. It was mad. Here I am *backstage* at Wireless but just twelve months before,

I was terrified to go up to the bar in case my card was declined. Now, I'm eating half a chicken and some peri-peri chips from the on-site Nando's – which was bangin' that they had one back-stage – watching the stars coming and going, surrounded by their entourages.

At one point I got separated from the friends I'd come with. I was on one side of the stage and all of my mates were on the other. Festival security had locked down backstage and weren't letting nobody pass through.

'Nah, sir, I'm sorry, you can't come in here,' the guy told me.

'Oh! I just need to get to my friends, over there!' I explained.

'We've got somebody coming out. I can't say who.'

'Please! I'll be really quick!' I begged.

He eventually gave in. 'Go on! But straight through …'

I quickly walked past him and, as I hurried along, I glanced over at an entrance to my right.

Drake was standing there. I looked at him and he looked at me. I nodded.

But then he walked up to me, with his huge entourage behind him.

'Wassup, Mo?' he asked.

'Yeah, yeah, good, man! How about yourself?' *I really did not know what to say here.* 'How's the … er, music?'

'It's going well, man. Hey, we've got an after-party later. You wanna come?'

'Yeah, I'll pass through,' I said, not wanting to sound as eager as I really was.

'OK, catch you later.' He nodded, sweeping towards the stage.

I made my way to the other side of the backstage in a bit of a daze. I saw a couple of people staring at me: *Shit! Drake and Mo know each other?* When I found my friends, Chris and Javan, they were as excited as I was.

After Drake played, we saw him again backstage and he said hello.

'Yo, Mo, good to see you again!'

He chatted to us, really friendly, just like a normal guy. He was so laid-back that we just relaxed around him and enjoyed ourselves. I was so impressed with his attitude. This guy is one of the BIGGEST stars in the world and it is all too easy to put celebrities like him on a pedestal, but he was just cool and down to earth.

It's funny – there was another American rapper at Wireless, I can't even remember his name, who was marching around backstage with five security guards. I looked at him, thinking, *Bro, I don't even know who you are! And you're acting like that!* But Drake, who was headlining the whole thing, was so chilled.

Drake also invited me to his album launch party in Mayfair, at a club called Annabel's, two days later. It was a mad party because bare people were just there walking around. Migos, French Montana, Wizkid, Giggs, Lily Allen ... it was sick, and everyone was having a great time. I had another chat with Drake and he was just as cool again.

His album was called *Scorpion* and all the party guests got given a custom jacket that said 'Scorpion' on it, with their name embroidered on the back.

I asked for a small one because I didn't want it to be too over-sized, but then when I picked it up, it was so little that I couldn't really wear it. I was a bit pissed off but ended up keeping it as a memento of a wicked night.

I mean, how pissed off could I be? I thought to myself: *Bruv, two years ago you were* selling *jackets! Now Drake is giving you one with your name on it! It's a mad, mad life …*

•   •   •

When the Vaudeville Theatre dates rolled around in October 2018, they were amazing. I had walked up and down The Strand so many times, in my youth and on nights out, and now *boom!* Here I was, playing in a proper West End theatre!

Just down the road was *The Lion King*, and here was my name and face, on big billboards, outside the theatre: *Mo Gilligan – The Coupla Cans Tour*. A Black British comic with his name up in lights! *My* name up in lights! I did a lot of pinching myself when I first saw it – and got a few pictures!

One really funny thing happened at one show. I was still coming out as the geezer character, then doing the roadman half-way through the night, then being myself after the interval. A director friend of mine came down. After the show, he got talking to a random woman from the audience.

'Great show, wasn't it?' he asked her.

'Yeah!' she replied. 'I really liked the guy right at the beginning – he was really good?'

'Er … that was Mo?' he said.

'No, no it wasn't!' she insisted. And wouldn't believe him that, yeah, it truly was.

The Vaudeville Theatre shows, like the Leicester Square shows, had sold out and went really well.

After that, we decided to take the tour overseas. All the way to Australia.

Taking the tour to Australia was amazing, and cool ... but also quite scary. In the UK, we'd had a bit of a crew: Kae to support, and a DJ, and a little road crew. On the twenty-four-hour journey to Australia, it was just me and the tour manager. Oh, and a persistent, nagging thought:

Is anybody going to come to see me?

I had no idea how much people knew about me in Australia. We had two shows planned – one in Melbourne, one in Sydney – and before the first date, I went on a TV show that filmed in Melbourne to try to promote them.

The show seemed a bit like a down-under version of *The One Show* and the presenter had a rather weird take on me. It seemed the guy had just seen me on *The Russell Howard Hour* and that was the end of his research, because when it came time to introduce me, he said:

'Now, all the way from England, we've got Mo Gilligan – who is a bit of a Rastafarian rapper!'

A Rastafarian rapper! That's the strangest introduction I've ever had. But when we had a chat, the guy was cool enough.

The Melbourne show was in a lovely little venue that held maybe two hundred people, but I had no idea what ticket sales were like. Before it started, I sat backstage. You can normally hear the buzz of the crowd getting settled, but this place sounded *dead silent*.

Shit! Nobody's here!

Then my tour manager appeared in my room backstage and started scooping up a few chairs that were standing around.

'What are you doing?' I asked him.

'We need more chairs!' he said. 'It's sold out, and there's not enough seats out there.'

Rah! That really hyped me up, and it ended up being a really sick show. Afterwards, I hung around and went out to meet some of the audience members who had stuck around for a drink.

'Great show, sport!' one of them told me.

'Thanks!' I said. 'Er, how did you know about me?'

'I saw you on television last night. But, hey, I thought you were a Rastafarian rapper?'

Melbourne seemed very like London to me – yeah, it was even raining – but Sydney was something else. Sydney was well sunny and felt oddly like America. I had a gawp at the Opera House and the Harbour Bridge then had to go for a lie-down in the hotel because it was so hot.

It was a much bigger venue than Melbourne and I had the same fear of not filling it, but it was sold out again. There were a lot of expats there keen to hear a London accent, but plenty of Aussies as well. The show went great, and afterwards I was buzzing: *I've sold out two shows in Australia! Not by being on TV – just on the back of what I've done online! Yes, I think I can make this comedy thing work . . .*

When I had started the tour, Ian from Live Nation had said to me, 'Just savour every moment. Enjoy it. You'll go on to bigger rooms, but your first tour will always be very special.' He was right. And it had been.

By the time the tour finally came to an end in late 2018, the tour had sold 50,000 tickets. *50,000 tickets!* It had been extended four times and lasted for eighteen months. Beyond my wildest expectations!

But what next? When you have achieved your dream, and done a huge tour that's gone as well as that, what do you do next?

Well, there's always television!

But, first, I needed a holiday ...

11

THAT MOMENT WHEN ...

The Mandem
Go To Vegas

In 2018, when *The Coupla Cans Tour* had ended, I could finally afford to take a break and have a holiday. I went on a mate's stag weekend to Las Vegas. And that meant that, beforehand, I had to immerse myself in the strange and unpredictable world of a lads' WhatsApp group chat.

Generally, the chances of guys ever getting it together to successfully plan a trip are about as good as those of teaching a goldfish to walk. You set up a holiday group to plan everything, but you hardly ever get as far as getting on a plane.

These are the main reasons why these much-discussed lads' holidays rarely come to fruition:

1. Laziness.
2. Prior engagements arranged by partners.
3. They can't decide whether it's a chilled break or a full-on sesh. The destination depends on what type of trip they want. Someone will suggest an obscure location such as Chernobyl because they heard about it on a podcast.
4. Work usually gets in the way for most of them – but, really, they secretly don't think this is a trip worth using those vital last five days of annual holiday for.

5. Point 1, again.
6. Lads' holiday group chats are far bigger on brainstorming than they are on making solid plans.
7. See Point 1, again.

Now, it takes a group of guys a long time to organise anything – particularly a holiday. Ideally, you should probably aim to start planning for it three years in advance and should fire up the WhatsApp group chat then!

I've seen so many big plans fail to materialise. One time, the mandem were planning to go to the 2014 World Cup in Brazil. Did we make it? *No.* Then, us same guys were also talking about the Olympics two years later. With exactly the same result ...

In fairness, we weren't the only ones. With these big events, lots of geezers have grand ideas about going to the next World Cup, Euros or Olympics. Getting tickets probably isn't as difficult as you might imagine, but what puts most people off is the hassle of actually organising it.

When these events are on the other side of the world, as they usually are, flights can get proper expensive. If you're serious about the trip, I always think it's best to put a deposit down because that just forces you to get on with it and plan everything.

According to the website Holidayhypemarket.co.uk, the current five favourite destinations for the best lads' holidays are:

- Cancun
- Ibiza

- Ayia Napa
- Tenerife
- Las Vegas

That sounds about right, doesn't it? There could maybe also be special mentions for Prague, Amsterdam and Berlin but that list is pretty accurate. Ibiza for the summer; Vegas, at some point, for someone's stag or big birthday.

· · ·

So, let's say you finally find yourself in a lads' holiday group chat. Great – that's a good start! But how do you go from there to the point where there is a group of you standing in Departures at Heathrow, waiting for the guy who's always late? (This time he forgot his passport and only realised once he'd got on the M25; he makes it just as the stewards are closing the plane doors.)

Firstly, the group chat needs someone to play centre midfield – the level-headed guy pulling all of the strings, driving the plans forward and holding it all together. On the complete other side of the spectrum, there's always that dreamer who suggests a wild plan ('Let's follow Route 66 and add on a week in LA!'), but he certainly won't be the one patient enough to track down the best flights and hotel deals.

If everyone is on board with the idea from the beginning, rather than semi-reluctant, there may even be a slight chance of the holiday going ahead. This is despite the inevitable long periods of silence in the group chat, as lads can't be arsed to get things sorted.

You normally go on your first lads' holiday when you are in your teens or early twenties. This often ends up being a bizarre one because no one has a clue what they're doing or has ever booked a holiday before. You end up on a Greek island that none of you have ever been to before, like Zante, Corfu or Kos.

Alternatively, you might finish up in a Spanish clubbing resort such as Ibiza or Magaluf. But those early lads' trips are rarely the holidays you want to repeat! One or two of them are enough for a lifetime!

By your mid- to late twenties, when you are still going on group holidays, at least everybody's earning a bit more money. Life's a bit more settled and it's probably the last time you'll all be hanging out before one or two of you start having kids. That's when you start picking your destinations and accommodation with more discretion. You've had enough of two-star hotels (and Airbnb always seems more cost-effective, anyway).

But, back to those early lads' holidays. If, by some miracle, you all manage to agree on dates, and everyone's been able to get their time off work, the next challenge is getting everyone to book the same flight. Sounds easy, right?

Think again! The guys who are the big ballers don't care as long as the plane defies gravity and gets them to Vegas – but the bargain hunters are the loudest in the group chat. For them, if getting to Vegas cheaply means three connecting flights and a camel ride across the Nevada Desert, so be it! Anything to save £100!

Whichever way you decide to get there, it'll still take ages for things to get booked. Group chats are basically just lads bantering, so there will be loads of memes, jokes and roasting slowing things down. If you're lucky, the banter may even be holiday related.

In the lead-up to the holiday, the banter intensifies. Everyone can't wait to get there ... but there's still one person that hasn't got his flights booked. Let's call him *Danny*. Danny's always Mr Last Minute: he hasn't booked his flight yet, but he swears he'll do it this week, as soon as he gets paid. He *will* make the holiday, just about, but he'll spend the whole time getting roasted for being late for everything.

There is also always somebody asking, 'Can somebody buy my ticket? I'll pay you back when I get paid, next week.' *Beware of that person!*

Days before the trip, happily nobody has pulled out, but the mode of transport to the airport has yet to be decided ... and some of the lads are suggesting a night out the night before the flight. Believe me, that isn't the smartest idea!

In any case, we might plan our holidays via a group chat but a weird thing about me is that I don't like arriving at the airport with someone else. I prefer making my own way there because for me, going on holiday has its own special ritual.

It starts with the packing. I often pack a couple of hours before the flight or, if I have a lot going on, I end up doing it at the last minute. But when you think about it, unless you're going backpacking for a year, or climbing Mount Everest, you don't really need that long to pack. It's not rocket science.

The most efficient holiday packers know that you don't take any more than what you need. There is a good rule of thumb:

if you are umming and ahhing about taking something because you're not too sure if you're going to wear it – trust me, you are definitely *not* going to wear it.

Well, I say that, but I'm afraid it's a case (a suitcase?) of do as I say, not as I do. I'm a serial over-packer. It pisses me off every single time I go on holiday and find myself carrying a stupidly heavy bag crammed with clothes that I probably wouldn't even wear at home.

Here's how my packing thought process goes: *I know I'm not going to wear this t-shirt but let me take it anyway, just in case ...*

And if I don't over-pack, I'll severely *under*-pack. I've done that a few times and found myself on holiday, pissed off at myself because I haven't got enough stuff with me. One time, I went on holiday to Spain without any trousers and had to go shopping for some.

Those Spanish trousers were not hitting! I don't really want to be buying clothes on holiday because, as well as wasting beach time, the sizes are all different – especially when you go to the States.

When it comes to boxers and socks, I over-pack those because ... well, *you just never know*. I love the black Supreme boxers and I buy a few new packs of them every year. They are so comfortable, they fit right and they just look nice, but I'll tell you one thing – I will *never* get a pair of white ones.

White boxers are criminal. You can just be going about your day, minding your business, having not even sat on the toilet all day – and you'll still find a skid mark in there.

It ruins the rest of your day, because you spend it revisiting the childhood trauma you had when your mum shouted at you because she found skid marks in your boxers when she was doing the washing. I mean, leaving skid marks in your boxers is bad enough – and now you're shaming yourself for it, as if you randomly decided to just take a shit in your most intimate item of clothing!

No, man. That can't run. No white boxer shorts for Mo!

My boxers are black and so are my T-shirts. I have tons of black T-shirts. As a performer you definitely go through more because you sweat buckets under the bright lights onstage. I like to shower and put on a fresh black T-shirt before every show. It's just my ritual. It's like how LeBron James used to clap the chalk at the scorer's table before every game, right?

But the hardest part of packing for a holiday is choosing which creps to take. That is like picking your favourite child! OK, your creps won't feel devastated if they're neglected, but we still think of them as our children! Or is that just me?

My deliberation process goes something like this:

- These creps haven't been out in time – they'll work great on holiday!
- Maybe I'll wear this pair one day, on an excursion …
- These creps will be for the nights, when I go out, and so will these ones – I want options …
- I might go to the gym, so I'll need these trainers …

Man, it's a proper long mental process, but I don't mind. There is an excitement in rushing around packing for holiday. After all, once you get away, you're free of deadlines and schedules. You're just packing to relax.

That's the strange thing. We're so used to running around every day that our holiday doesn't begin till the moment that we step on the plane. For a lot of people, it doesn't begin even then, because work still finds its way on the trip. It is the stowaway that nobody ever asks for.

I do like to take my gadgets, though. It's a bit annoying: I end up taking my Nintendo Switch, headphones, portable speakers, iPad and laptop. I always know that if I don't take the laptop, at some point I'll be fuming because I'll need it. There is always that one thing that you can't do on an iPad or an iPhone.

By the time you have all got to the airport, the group chat is relegated to simply being used for arranging meeting points during the holiday. The only thing is, you have forgotten to use it to arrange one important aspect of the lads' holiday: the itinerary.

Or, rather, the lack of it.

Guys just don't *do* itineraries. There might be one planned big night out, perhaps because there's a specific DJ playing that weekend in Ibiza, or there happens to be a big fight on in Vegas. Even then, you kind of know that your mate who 'knows someone' will fail to get the tickets and you'll all end up watching the fight on TV in the hotel bar. (Well, that's fine: no one at home will know either way, so lie away on the 'gram! If Bow Wow can lie about having a private jet, you can fib about going to that Tyson Fury fight!)

Then again, a trip to Vegas doesn't really require much of an itinerary, especially if you're not planning to do more than do a bit of gambling, go clubbing and check out a few shows. At heart, it's just an expensive piss-up in the middle of a desert. *What could possibly go wrong?*

Having no itinerary is also good because if there are a lot of you, it gives you the freedom to go off roaming in smaller subgroups some nights. It also gives you a better chance of getting into most clubs, whereas big groups end up waiting two hours for Leon while he does his press-ups in the hotel room to get swollen for the night out.

The group chat dies down when you are actually on holiday – why would you need it? You're all together! It only really comes alive again at the end of the trip, when everyone wants to relive the funniest moments.

But once that's passed, naturally the group chat dies. Everybody leaves, one by one, till one man's left standing because he's too busy to check WhatsApp (that's normally me). I think I'm still in WhatsApp groups from 2017.

• • •

I went to Vegas in 2018 for my mate Zac's stag do. Zac had made it clear for months that Vegas was what he wanted. I loved that because some of my favourite films, like *The Hangover* and *Casino*, are set in Vegas. And, against all the odds, we actually managed to make it happen.

The year before, the guys had gone to Miami but I couldn't go with them. I couldn't really afford it at the time, because I couldn't get the time off from the shop. So, this time, I thought I might as well go all out and flex.

It's a Vegas stag! You have to do it!

Our mate Liam took on the role I talked about earlier of looking for the cheapest flights. Liam will always find a deal, no matter where you're going.

The danger with looking for cheaper flights is there's normally a catch. No, forget *normally*. Make that *always*. It ends up being a twenty-hour flight with two stopovers, and your seat is somewhere on the wing.

So, what happened? Liam found return flights for £800, including hotel! We're all thinking that it's a fantastic deal till we notice that it has a connecting flight. From Canada. Not to mention a six-hour wait before the final four-hour flight from Canada to Vegas.

We binned that plan off.

I need to be comfortable when I'm flying. I really felt like this was the first holiday I was going all out on. It wasn't that money was no object – far from it! – but I was more concerned about having an enjoyable, memorable trip.

In any case, we wanted to stay in a proper Vegas hotel, as well. You *can't* go to Vegas and just stay in a random Hilton! It has to be one of the casino hotels: the MGM, Bellagio or the Venetian. There's a reason why they tend to be a little more expensive and that's because you're getting the full Vegas experience! So, we stayed at the Cosmopolitan, which was cool.

Of course, there will be somebody in the group chat who goes through five hundred reviews of the hotel on TripAdvisor to find the only negative one:

'★ Hated the hotel. We found a mouse in the room!'

These reviews are often left by old, rich pensioners on a trip to see the Grand Canyon.

Vegas is one of those holidays where you need to take money. (It's like Ibiza.) They're not places you can go on a budget, though many have tried. You want to have enough for raving, eating, excursions to the Grand Canyon and, obviously, gambling.

The whole point of us going to Vegas was that we were there to flex. Well, that was the plan, anyway …

•　•　•

We got to Vegas in the afternoon and the airport seemed absolutely dead. We got a couple of taxis and the first thing we did was ask the cab driver if we could go to the nearest liquor store to get our pre-drinks.

'Yeah, no problem!' the cabbie said. He had a look on his face that said we weren't the first cheapskate Brits ever to have put this request to him.

In the liquor store, each of us bought a bottle to take to the hotel. I grabbed a three-litre bottle of Captain Morgan that came with a hook. *A hook!* I had never seen anything like that before! What was I supposed to do with it – and is it really wise to be giving *hooks* to guys who are planning to drink three gallons of rum?! The crazy thing is it only cost me $20! Alcohol is mad cheap in America.

At the hotel, we started sorting out the rooms. Me and a mate ended up getting two rooms that were connected to each other, so our rooms became the vibe, the hub, for the whole trip.

He's my mate but it's not as though I've lived with him, so I didn't really know what he was like in terms of tidiness.

I'm quite organised when it comes to unpacking when I first arrive and, luckily, he turned out to be the same. He even went a little bit extra and started putting everything on hangers and his clothes in the drawers.

Hangers?! Steady on! I'm not in retail anymore!

The good thing about being in Vegas is that you can – in theory, at least – win back the money you have spent on the holiday. We were there for four nights so I figured it might even be achievable.

We headed to a casino and were putting down $25 bets, just to test the water. Before we went, I'd heard this story that you get free drinks in the gambling rooms at Vegas, so I was all up for that!

Sadly, for us, it turned out to be an urban legend.

I'd never been on a roulette table, so I didn't know how it worked. The closest I'd come to gambling before that was playing 'money up' (or 'pound up') in school – where a group of kids throw a pound each, and the closest one to the wall wins the lot. So, a Vegas casino was a new world for me!

As we were sitting at the table, I was asking questions as the game went along because I didn't really have a clue what I was doing. All I knew was what I'd seen in movies: you're betting on red or black.

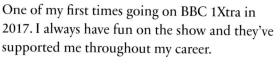

One of my first times going on BBC 1Xtra in 2017. I always have fun on the show and they've supported me throughout my career.

Feeling like a superstar at my first big awards show, the BET Awards 2017, with Don't Jealous Me and Daps.

Rubbing shoulders with the likes of Tosin Cole, Stormzy and Bashy at the GRM Daily Rated Awards 2017.

MO GILLIGAN

AKA MO THE COMEDIAN

COUPLA CANS TOUR 2017

OCTOBER

THU 5TH
OXFORD
O₂ ACADEMY

FRI 6TH
LIVERPOOL
O₂ ACADEMY

SAT 7TH
BIRMINGHAM
O₂ ACADEMY

SUN 8TH
BRISTOL
MR WOLFS

WED 11TH
HULL
FRUIT

THU 12TH
LEICESTER
DRYDEN STREET SOCIAL

SUN 15TH
MANCHESTER
GORILLA

WED 18TH
LONDON
PROUD CAMDEN

WED 25TH
BRIGHTON
KOMEDIA

THE UK'S FASTEST RISING
SOCIAL MEDIA STAR ON HIS
DEBUT UK TOUR!

LIVE NATION PRESENTATION IN ASSOCIATION WITH ARTIST MANAGEMENT

MOTHECOMEDIAN   MOTHECOMEDIAN   MOGILLI

My first ever tour poster, before we added a gazillion more dates.

One of my biggest shows, at Birmingham O2 Academy, playing to 1,000 people. Here I am as one of my characters, the Roadman.

o₂ academy

54909861736960

LIVE NATION & UTC PRESENTS
MO GILLIGAN – COUPLA CANS
CHARITY SPECIAL

16+
UNDER 25S REQUIRE ID TO BUY ALCOHOL
CURFEW 23:00

O2 SHEPHERD'S BUSH EMPIRE
SHEPHERD'S BUSH GREEN
LONDON
W12 8TT

THU 13-DEC-18 DOORS 19:00

LEVEL 1   ROW A SEAT 3   COMP

ZZZ GUEST COMPS
PRICE 0.00 S/C   FACILITY FEE 0.00 TOTAL 0.00
COMP   4624 AME601   13DEC18 16:55 CN 59337

Seeing my name up in lights for the first time at the Vaudeville Theatre is something I'll never forget.

Getting a Coupla Cans in before the show at O2 Academy Liverpool.

A charity show we added, where we raised £15k for three charities: Brixton Soup Kitchen, ACLT, and Shelter.

I never stop laughing when working with Big Narstie on *The Big Narstie Show.*

Presenting a BAFTA in 2019 with Lolly Adefope and making sure not to touch the award so as not to jinx my luck!

Getting my red carpet moment in my Hugo Boss suit at the GQ Awards 2018.

Getting ready to film the first episode of *The Lateish Show* with the legendary Tyson Fury as one of my first guests.

Already feeling at home on my new show.

Meeting Jada was such a big highlight for me, even if I did have to tell her to re-pick the competition winner for the show!

Rehearsing my Netflix special for the big show later that day – I was really nervous but excited!

The calm before the storm, right before we opened the doors.

Winning my BAFTA was a huge moment – I just couldn't stop laughing I was so shocked!

It was an honour to work with incredible comedians such as Angie Le Mar for my documentary: *Black, British and Funny*.

The Masked Singer is one of the most fun things I've gotten to work on, made even more so by people like the brilliant Joel Dommett.

Driving round in a taxi with my face on the front was a whole different kind of experience! I'm looking forward to finally getting this show on the road in 2021. Get ready, world – here I come!

Vegas casinos are mad. They have no windows, and I've heard rumours they pump in oxygen to keep people awake and betting! People are hunched over tables, looking stressed and intense. Others can be having the time of their lives, laughing away, while some poor guy is gambling off his kid's tuition fund. I think some casinos even give you massages at the tables.

It was St Patrick's Day weekend, which also fell over spring break, so the Cosmopolitan casino was doing serious business. I exchanged $50 for two chips. A rowdy group of American guys watching the table were telling me to bet on black, because it was hot that night. So, I put $25 on black, the dealer spun the wheel and dropped in the ball.

I watched it bounce between the numbers – red, black, red, red, black, black – feeling like I just threw $25 down the gutter. After all, the house always wins.

It landed on black.

I was so gassed! *I'm up!*

I put down another $25 chip.

Black again.

I'm up $50!

I started putting down $50 instead. Everyone was getting convinced that black was hot on this table, and more people started to crowd around and place their bets on black.

Another British guy came along and put some money on red. He lost his bet and the American guys let him have it.

'I told you, man! You shoulda put it on black, like these guys have been doing!'

It went wicked, like a dream! I ended up making $450 from that initial bet of $25! I treated one of my friends to a trip to Taco Bell (yeah, yeah, I know how to celebrate!). When we get back to the hotel, I walked into my mate's room, saying 'I've just won $450!'

Everyone in our party was in the room and I thought they'd be excited for me, but they seemed surprised more than anything. They asked me how I'd done it.

I explained how I won it playing roulette. Then I realised that there was a bit of a conference going on in the room because one of our friends – *we'll call him Rob* – had run out of money and we were planning to go out that night.

Another big problem with guys' holidays is that someone always runs out of money. It was a problem because the club table we had booked was going to cost the rest of us more now, because Rob didn't have any money to chip in.

It's not that we minded helping him out. Obviously, we weren't gonna leave him in the hotel room.

But, hearing about my winning streak, one of the guys had a brainwave that we could help Rob win some money on the roulette table ...

What could possibly go wrong?

So, armed with only $100, eleven of us went down to the casino floor. I don't know what was in the air that night – maybe there was a leprechaun looking down on us or something, sprinkling us with good-luck dust – but I'm telling you, we cleaned up. We walked away with $5,000 each!

We went out clubbing with our wads of cash and got to hang out with Steven Aoki backstage, where we met Mike Tyson and Jerry Seinfeld! Steve invited us to his after-party, where he threw a cake in my friend's face. Celine Dion was there too, and she invited us to her show the next evening. It was hands-down the greatest night of our lives, the kind of story we would tell our children, and their children …

It's also a complete lie.

We did go gambling to try to win Rob some spending money, but this is how it actually went down …

We decided to give it a go the next day. That night all the mandem got on their phones and started googling tips and strategies to win at roulette.

The next day, back on the table, I got lucky again. I had changed my tactics and was betting on red. It had been landing on red nearly every time and I was up again, by $300. I'd even come up with my own slogan: 'Put it on red and there's no blood shed!'

After a few more wins, I decided to cash out.

Meanwhile, Rob was $25 up and umming and ahing over what bet to place next. I advised him to put $25 on red.

It landed on red.

He was up $50! I convinced him to put down another $25.

Yep, red again!

Rob was up $75 by this point. He wanted to bet again. I stuck to the same advice: 'Put it on red and there's no blood shed!'

It landed on black.

Rob was back down to $50 and was getting stressed. I told him maybe he should cash out now. But he went ahead and bet on red, lost again, then he started to blame me.

'Why did you tell me to put it on red?!'

'It's your money!' I told him. 'You can put it on whatever you want!'

Rob was pissed off by now. And we were all thinking that maybe he shouldn't be betting any more, because he was holding his last $25 chip.

But he wasn't stopping now.

'Place your bets!' said the dealer.

Rob put his chip on black.

The dealer spun the wheel. 'No more bets!'

The ball teetered over black ... and then, at the last second, dropped onto red.

And Rob lost it, big time! He shouted at the dealer, the casino and the world in general:

'Fuck this game and suck your mum!'

I can still hear those words, and his voice, right now, echoing around my head! Man, it was the funniest thing I had ever seen! We were all laughing like little schoolboys! Rob was so stressed that he stormed off from the table.

When he'd cooled off, Rob eventually saw the funny side of it. And guess what? He still came with us to the pool party that afternoon and let us pay for him all day ... and the rest of the trip.

12

THAT MOMENT WHEN ...

Big Narstie Needs to Go Toilet. Now!

While *The Coupla Cans Tour* was going on, I had started to move more into television. I'd done a little bit before, like *The Johnny and Inel Show* on CBBC and, ahem, the Rastafarian nursery rhymes on *The Russell Howard Hour*. But I knew that I wanted to get more exposure on telly.

Polly and I went to lots of meetings. I'd do five-minute stand-up sets at comedy and television showcase events at the Soho Theatre in the West End. They were like a roll call of up-and-coming talent for people who run production companies and commission shows on TV.

We were going to development meetings at networks and with production companies, and it would feel like something was about to happen, but it *never* did. I'd head off to the middle of nowhere to film a sketch … then hear nothing. At times it would feel frustrating.

Things started to ramp up while I was on *The Coupla Cans Tour*, which I first started to notice when I was onstage. I'd do the little bit where I'd banter with the first couple of rows in the audience and get a bit of chat going. I'd ask one of my standard questions:

'Hello, mate, what do you do?'

'I work in television.'

Oh! We'd have a bit of banter, then I'd ask another guy:

'And what do you do for a job?'

'I work at the BBC.'

There were a couple of nights where I'd ask people at random, and it seemed like everybody worked in TV. I thought to myself, *Hmm. We've got a lot of these TV types coming down here! Where are all the people who do a regular nine-to-five?*

Polly started telling me in advance when television people were coming down to see me. She'd say *this* executive or *that* producer was going to be in that night. It was good to know ... but I didn't want to get distracted by them being there, which had happened before when I knew somebody important was coming down to watch me and I had felt as if I was perform-ing the show just to *them*. I didn't want that. I wanted to go on and perform to the real audience: the people who had *paid* for their tickets.

So, I'd do my normal show, and then I'd meet the TV execs backstage afterwards, and they would say, 'That was great, Mo – can we do lunch?'

I started getting taken for a *lot* of lunches and it became a bit of a ritual. Don't get me wrong – a very *nice* ritual! We'd get invited to a nice restaurant, really fancy places. I'd turn up, proba-bly in a tracksuit, and eat some seriously delicious food while the execs said their piece.

Basically, they were trying to woo me.

I suppose it's like when footballers get tapped up. *'Yeah, he had lunch with Mourinho, then he signed for Tottenham!'* The TV people would have ideas for me, which we'd chat about over a steak and some chips that'd cost £50. Some of the ideas made sense to me. Some of them didn't. The fancy food and drink at least made it easier to listen to their mad ideas.

There was one particular night that I played the Clapham Grand early on during my first tour. It was a mad night because a lot of people that I knew were coming down. Krept & Konan were there, so was Michael Dapaah. Tinie Tempah turned up in a Maybach!

MC Neat was there, which was weird for me, having grown up on old-school garage. He'd brought his son along too. Katie Piper was in the house, as well as Maisie Williams from *Game of Thrones*. I think Jermain Defoe, the footballer, was also there.

All of those people were there – at my show! –and Polly told me a lot of TV people were coming down too. Proper important people from all of the networks, who'd each been given a box of their own to watch the show from. There were producers from the BBC, ITV, Sky … and Channel 4.

I don't know why, but it was Channel 4 that excited me the most then. Of all the meetings Polly and I had gone to, the ones with them had felt the most promising.

So, with friends, celebs *and* major TV people there, it could have been a seriously high-pressure gig … but it went amazingly well. It was a *wicked* show, one of those that just flows right from start to finish. Every joke seemed to hit and the audience were in hysterics all night.

It was one of those nights that comics dream of. I remember walking off the stage at the end, after the encore, grinning myself stupid and thinking, *Phoof! That was a good one!* I got back to my dressing room, then Polly knocked on the door.

'Channel 4 loved it! They want you to come in for a meeting,' she said. 'As soon as possible. This week.'

A day or two later, Polly and I went down to the Channel 4 HQ in central London. It was a place that meant something to me, because it was round the corner from my secondary school, and every now and then I'd walk past it. So, it was nice to go in, get given a pass and head upstairs.

We had had a couple of meetings at Channel 4 before, but we had always known in advance what they were about. This one? Polly hadn't got a clue. All she had been told was that they wanted to see me.

I thought they might be about to offer me a trial show on E4. Or maybe even just to make a pilot. I would have been happy with that: *anything* would have been good, really. We waited outside an office and then we got called in to see Becky Cadman, a Factual Entertainment Commissioner, and Syeda Irtizaali, the Entertainment Commissioner.

We walked into a plush meeting room.

'It's great to meet you, Mo!' Syeda said. 'I just want to say, I loved your show. I thought it was amazing!'

'Thank you,' I said, a little embarrassed. I never know how to take people's compliments. 'I really appreciate that.'

'I think you have a huge future in entertainment,' she continued. 'And I think you're gonna be absolutely massive. That's why I've asked you to come in here today.'

I was thinking, *Man, she is saying some seriously nice things! Where is this leading?*

'Mo I would like to offer you the chance to have your own show, on Channel 4, on Friday nights at ten o'clock.'

I looked at Polly.

Polly looked at me.

Time stood still but Syeda wasn't finished …

'There's something else,' she said. 'We're also doing a show with Big Narstie, which we'll get going with quite soon. We'd like you to be the co-host on that.'

My reply was … well … I'd love to pretend that I came back with something suave, sophisticated, elegant and laid-back. I actually said:

'*SHIT!!!*'

I knew I shouldn't have sworn and apologised straight away to Syeda, who was laughing her head off. But it was just too much for me to take in. My mind was racing: Had she really just said that? Had she really just given me a show at ten o'clock on Friday nights on Channel 4? *Me, Mosiah Gilligan from south London? I'm going to be on two Channel 4 shows?*

'Yes!' I said, very quickly. 'Yes, please! I would love to.'

I was in a daze as Syeda carried on talking. She was saying that my show would take a little while to plan and get off the ground, so it wouldn't get broadcast till the following year. But

Narstie's show was more advanced, and I could start work on that straight away.

Then, Syeda said something else, equally mad, to me.

'Of course, we want you to find the right production company to make your show.'

What?

Being allowed to choose your own production company is huge! I felt as if I had just been offered the keys to the kingdom at Channel 4. And, basically, I had.

Polly and I left Channel 4 as if we were walking on air. We hugged each other: *Shit! Did that really just happen?* After, Polly went back to the office while I just went walking, on my own, around central London, with a million thoughts in my head.

What I was thinking was: *Wow! My life just changed forever!* Because I knew that going on Channel 4 with two – *two!* – shows would change everything in my career, and my life. Nothing would ever be the same again.

I'll never forget that day – 16 December 2017. It was a disgustingly grey day, but I hardly noticed the weather. All I was thinking about was how I had left retail, started my first tour and gone to the BET Awards in that same year.

I wandered on, not knowing what to do with myself. Then I stopped and took a deep breath. It was time to get to work.

First on the agenda was *The Big Narstie Show.*

• • •

The first thing I had to do was obvious: go and meet Big Narstie! Obviously, I knew all about him from the grime scene, and his

Uncle Pain DVDs, but I hadn't met him before. As it happened, I was to have a chance encounter almost straight away.

I was asked to do a little commercial job when they launched the new *Call of Duty*. I was hired to make people laugh while they played the game at the launch. I thought, *Yeah, cool, I can do that – it should be fun!*

And, as it happens, Big Narstie was there.

I noticed him straight away – bruv, he is kind of hard to miss! He was talking to a guy next to him.

'Yeah, blud, man's got his own TV show, you get me?' he was saying.

I joined the conversation:

'Cool, cool, that's great!'

Narstie went on:

'Yeah, BBC and Channel 4 are fighting over it ...'

Huh? Narstie clearly wasn't caught up on the news I would be his co-host. Then again, he is a guy who partakes in 'herbal reme- dies', so I could understand how he would forget ... but I didn't say anything then. We just swapped a bit of banter and I carried on working the room.

The next week, he and I had a meeting at Expectation Produc- tion Company. Narstie turned up with all his entourage and we all sat at a couple of long tables, on opposite sides of the room, to talk about the show.

Now, I'm always very vocal in meetings like that. I've always got a ton of ideas and I like to share them. So, every chance I got, I was saying, 'So, I think we should do *this* ...' and 'Let's not do *that* ...' and 'You know what, though? I think *this* might work ...'

Every time I looked over, I could just see Narstie staring at me, like: *Where's Mo going with all these ideas?*

It was a good brainstorming meeting, though. And after that, our next job was to film the pilot.

• • •

When we came to do it, it was *massive*. There must have been five hundred people in the audience, which is unheard of for a pilot. Narstie, the rest of the team and I had been working on the show for weeks – a lot of early mornings and late nights. We'd written some great bits and got some special guests in: Tinie Tempah, Rylan Clark-Neal and Victoria Coren Mitchell.

We'd smashed it out the park. The audience was in hysterics and Channel 4 was fully on board; before we knew it, they went ahead and officially announced *The Big Narstie Show.*

Here we go!

Next, we had to film the opening trails for the programme, where we're in our suits and they get ripped off and we're in our normal clothes. We did it in Lewisham and, man, it was *loooong*. I had got a real bad migraine and the filming seemed to go on forever.

It was *stop. Start. Stop. Start. Cut! Do another take! Stop. Start.* And my head felt like it was gonna burst. *Stop. Start. Cut!* I was saying, 'Come on, my head hurts! Can we just do this, please, and go home?' But Narstie just started laughing. And when Narstie laughs, he don't stop!

Narstie and I had great chemistry from the start. We had an instant rapport and similar interests. I respected what he'd done, and I think he respected what I was doing with my comedy. We were cool with each other. Sometimes we had so much fun we forgot we were making a TV show.

We were always cussin' each other. It felt like I was just hanging out with one of my mates.

As soon as we got going, Narstie was cussin' my skinny jeans and I was cussin' his bootcut jeans. People liked it because they could see we were having fun, and with my comedy background, I loved it. I'd been cussin' people since the back of the school bus!

We had one rule, though: mums were off limits. The last thing we wanted to do was stand there cussin' each other's mums on national TV.

Narstie is a very smart guy. People might think he is just a big dude larking around, but he built himself a huge reputation doing things like Uncle Pain and his guest spot delivering the weather on *Good Morning Britain*. While we were writing the show, he was dropping some serious mad wisdom.

Our on-screen relationship got established from the very first *The Big Narstie Show*. Narstie came out through the audience, milked the applause, said a few words and then introduced me like this:

'This is my coleslaw to my main Nando's dish – Mo Gilligan!'

We'd take the piss out of each other, but then in the week we'd be in the writers' room, thinking up ideas for sketches. Some of the ideas Narstie would come out with were so funny! They'd make no sense but they'd be funny and he'd be so serious about them.

We did a sketch called *Grime & Prejudice*, vibing off Jane Austen's *Pride & Prejudice*. Narstie and me were in period costume in a posh drawing room, talking to two aristocratic ladies but doing it in proper grime, street style:

> NARSTIE: We've been to a gentlemen's club. The array of
>   tun-tun was vastly disappointing!
> ME: What we needed was a Coupla Karens!

Then, later, as we challenged each other to a duel:

> ME: My G! You want to do this now?
> NARSTIE: I do, my G! I am no rasclaat bumble clat fuckin'
>   eejet, man!

The sketch got loads of laughs and people shared it on socials a lot, so the next week Channel 4 said, 'That was great – can you do something else like it this week?'

OK, cool! We had guests from *Love Island* that week, so in the writers' room, we were trying to think of a theme around that. I said, 'Why don't we call it *Bruv Island*?'

'Nah, nah!' said Narstie. 'Why don't we just call it *Grime & Prejudice Island*?' And he was serious!

'No, Narstie, man!' I tried to explain. 'That was a play on *Pride & Prejudice*, and now we need a play on *Love Island* ...'

'What's the problem, though?' he asked. 'They liked that one last week, yeah, so just call it *Grime & Prejudice Island*, you get me?'

I love it when that happens! I sit and explain things to Narstie and he just stares at me, then suddenly he gets it and goes 'Ah, OK, OK, OK!' And his face is so funny! Man, we'll be dying of laughter in the writers' room.

Recording the show can be hysterical. We're all having a laugh, and Narstie might be jumping about and throwing Haribo into the audience – it just feels like messing about with your mates. We could make another full show every week from the bits that don't make the final edit.

Narstie is just himself all the time. 100% himself. I remember once we were recording a big sketch, and halfway through, he just said: 'I need to go toilet! Right now!'

Huh?

The producer was saying, 'We really need to record this link first ...'

'I don't give a fuck!' said Narstie. 'I'm going toilet!' And off he went, there and then.

I like that. Television can be a serious business, so it's fun to see a bit of anarchy like that. Someone saying, 'I'm going toilet – now!'

I got to know very quick what Narstie would do and what he wouldn't. I got used to his ways. One day I was in a meeting with a producer, and he said, 'I've got this idea where Narstie comes in on a skateboard ...'

'Uh-uh.' I interrupted him. 'I'll tell you now – Narstie won't do that. Forget it.'

'It'll be great!' the producer persisted. 'I'm going to ask him.'

'OK, you do that …'

Narstie got to the meeting and sat himself down. The producer spoke to him: 'Hey, Narstie, we're going to have you coming in on a skateboard …'

'No, fuck that, bruv,' said Narstie, in a totally matter-of-fact way.

And I gave the producer that look that says, *'I told you so …'*

Maybe Narstie and me seemed like the maddest combination at first, but as the show went on, people got what my role was. Narstie is wicked funny but he can be pretty, let's say, 'out there', and it's sometimes my job to keep things together. But the beauty of the show, for me, is I still get the chance to showcase my comedy as well.

I've sat along the sofa from some crazy-famous guests. One minute I could be talking to Nile Rodgers about Studio 54 while the next I'd be chatting to Manchester United Legend Rio Ferdinand. It's been hard to believe. When we're talking, I'm always concentrating on holding things together and keeping the conversation moving, so some weeks it's not till I watch the show back on TV that I think: *Shit! I'm talking to some absolute legends!*

I mean, we had Dennis Rodman on – *Dennis Rodman!* – and he started to cry when Narstie asked him about the response he got in America when he started hanging out with Kim Jong-Un in North Korea, and Dennis said his family got death threats. It's mad, when you think about it.

David Schwimmer came on one week. We were sitting on the sofa after we'd filmed, and I said, 'Ah, I'm going to New York next weekend with my girlfriend!'

'Oh, really?' asked David. 'You want to meet up and have lunch?'

Seriously? Ross from Friends *is inviting me to Central Perk for some lunch?*

And a week later, I was sitting in Manhattan across a dining table from David Schwimmer. That was sick.

The Big Narstie Show was a great first introduction to television for me because it was just such fun to do. I would go into work and just laugh and laugh and laugh. And also, in a special sort of way, it felt kind of important.

One thing that I liked from the start is that it is unapologetically a show by Black people for Black people. It's nice to be in a show like that for a new generation who normally wouldn't ever see themselves portrayed on TV. They can totally relate to it.

I'll never forget the morning after the first show got broadcast. My girlfriend and I went out to get some breakfast and a woman about my sister's age approached me with her son.

'Oh my God, I seen you on TV last night!' she said. 'I seen you on *The Big Narstie Show* – it was great!'

'Thanks! That means a lot!' I said.

'I'm so proud of you!' she went on. 'I've got two young boys and I don't let them stay up to watch TV, but I let them watch you last night because they don't normally see people who look like us on television.'

Then it was *my* turn to feel proud. Because it was a very cool moment.

The Big Narstie Show was the first regular mainstream telly I'd done, which naturally led to me being recognised in the street like that a lot more. Except that, sometimes it wasn't in the street – and the person doing the recognising was far more famous than me.

• • •

In September 2018, a friend who had designed a football boot invited me to watch Arsenal play Watford from a box with him. I'd never been in a box at a football match before. It was a great day – we got given free sushi, and Arsenal won 2–0 (an own goal and one from Özil). *Rah!*

After the game, I was talking to some guy when there was a commotion down the far end of the box. You know how you can sense it when somebody more important comes in a room? The geezer I was talking to just said, 'Sorry, gotta go!' and dashed down there.

Huh? I looked down the room to see that it was ... Ian Wright! He had everybody clustered around him, wanting to talk to him and get selfies, and truth is, I felt a little shy to go up to him. So, I stayed where I was, till I heard a voice boom down the room:

'Mo! Oh, man, it's Mo Gilligan! Mo, come over here!'

And the booming voice was coming from ... Ian Wright! He was beaming, beckoning me over and doing his big *Match of the Day* laugh:

'I love this guy, man!'

I went over, nervously, and he gave me a big hug.

'What's going on, man?' Ian asked me. 'I'm a big fan of your stuff!'

I got a selfie with him and was buzzing so much (I decided not to mention our previous meeting, when I was working in Jo Malone)!

That evening I went on *The Jonathan Ross Show* and sat along-side Olly Murs, Noel Fielding, Paul Hollywood and Prue Leith to talk about *The Coupla Cans Tour*, *The Big Narstie Show* and my own upcoming TV show. It was one of the best days of my life – and I was getting a lot of clues life was changing beyond all recognition …

. . .

When *The Big Narstie Show* first aired, it felt like a bit of a moment. There was a resurgence of grime music going on, *Top Boy* was big on TV, and actors like Daniel Kaluuya were doing movies like *Get Out*. It felt like we were a part of the young Black voices getting heard.

The people the show was aimed at *got* it from the start, and the critics seemed to like it as well. The first series got nominated for a couple of awards – and the first one was the Royal Television Society, or RTS, Awards.

That was a mad night.

We were filming an episode of the show that day, so as soon as we finished, I got put on a fast motorbike to the awards show at the Grosvenor House Hotel on Park Lane. We were zooming through the London traffic – it felt like proper James Bond stuff!

We were up for Best Entertainment Performance against two other nominees: *Michael McIntyre's Big Show* and Jennifer Hudson on *The Voice*. We got there, sat down, had some nice dinner ... and we won!

Woah! It felt fantastic to win and it was such a funny night. I got dressed up in a tux for the night, and Narstie turned up in ... a tracksuit covered in teddy bears. After we got our award, we had to go and talk to the press.

They were asking us, 'How are you guys feeling? You must be pumped that you've won?'

I said, 'Yeah, it's nice to win! It's a great thing for us, but also for all the people who work on the show and for the viewers as well.'

Well, that was me. Narstie took a more unconventional approach to the press questioning.

'Done now. Come on!' he said, as he sat there in his teddy bears. 'BDL every day, you get me? First of all, gotta big-up Jah Jah! Big-up Jah, you get me? And fucking ... big-up everybody else, innit?'

I could see the journalists looking at each other, like, *Huh?*

Winning the RTS Awards was great, and very soon after that, we got nominated for the big one ... a BAFTA.

When we heard about that, I was like, *Oh my gosh, this is huge!* Because BAFTA is the all-important TV academy, and not many shows get nominated for their first series. Man, there are great shows that have been around a *long* time and have never got nominated for a BAFTA!

And not only were we up for a BAFTA – they asked me to present an award as well! *Woah!*

It felt like a massive deal to me, so I wanted to get myself a wicked blazer for the awards. *Rah! Let's get a tuxedo blazer!* I'm not gonna lie – I thought as well as going to the BAFTAs, maybe I might make the best-dressed list!

I found one that I liked online and went to Harrods. Annoyingly, they didn't have it in stock and I couldn't see anything else that I liked. So, I walked around and then stumbled across … Tom Ford.

Tom Ford! Oh my gosh! I walked over, thinking, *Let's just go and have a browse.* And as I was mooching around in my hoodie and tracksuit bottoms, an assistant glided over to talk to me.

'Do you need any help, sir?'

'Yeah, I'm looking for a blazer,' I said.

'Do you mind if I ask what it's for?'

'I'm going to the BAFTAs!' (I didn't think that was a line I'd ever say to someone while I was buying a blazer!)

'Then let me show you some of these pieces, sir …'

The guy was so nice – I was getting proper *Pretty Woman* customer service – the good kind, after Richard Gere lends her some cash! He showed me a great green blazer, and I knew straight away this was the one I wanted. It needed a few alterations but he told me not to worry, they'd sort it all out for me; free of charge.

Now I had my Tom Ford blazer, I felt ready for the BAFTAs … but unfortunately at the last minute Narstie wasn't able to make it.

Turning up at the awards at the Royal Festival Hall was exciting, even if nobody really wanted to talk to me on the red carpet.

Yet when I got in, sat down and looked around … it was funny. I had real mixed feelings.

I didn't feel like the mandem were there with me. There were a few people that I knew: Tosin Cole from *Doctor Who*; Samson Kayo and Tommy Moutchi, who were in *Famalam* … but it didn't feel like there were many people from my community alongside me. In a funny way, I felt like I was there by myself.

The Big Narstie Show was up for Best Comedy and Entertainment Programme against *The Last Leg*, *A League of Their Own* and *Would I Lie to You?* It was the first award to get presented on the night and my head was in a whirl.

They had sat me right at the front, by the stairs to the stage, which made me wonder – *Is that to make it easy for me to go up and collect it?* And it was to be presented by David Schwimmer – was that another clue?

Or was I just imagining it?

I had scribbled down a few lines, just in case, and I thought if we won, I might go up and FaceTime Narstie from the stage. That was all going through my head. The host, Graham Norton, called David Schwimmer and comedy actor Nick Mohammed onstage – and a cameraman came and stuck his camera right in my face.

Shit! We might even win this!

My heart was beating so loud, I thought they might hear it on the stage! That camera was in my face as they rolled the VT packages of the nominees. David Schwimmer opened the envelope, and Nick Mohammed said:

'The winner is … *A League of Their Own!*'

Ah, well! I was sitting clapping, and the camera was still focusing on me! I didn't know what I was supposed to do – look at the camera? Ignore it? *Why was it still there?*

Almost as soon as it got announced, I had to go backstage to wait to present an award. I looked around and was surrounded by people that I watch on telly. I saw Ant and Dec, who I had been watching ever since I was a kid from when they were on *Byker Grove*!

I didn't know what to do. I wanted to go up to them and say, 'Hi, nice to meet you guys! Big up, I've been watching you forever!' But at the same time, I didn't want to be a fanboy. I managed to say, 'What's up, guys? You alright? Nice to meet you, man!' and they were really friendly.

I saw Sir Lenny Henry, as well. He is somebody that definitely influenced me when I was younger. It wasn't because I knew that I was going to be a comedian, or anything like that. It was more that he was one of the few famous Black people you saw on TV back in the 1990s and early 2000s.

I knew that Lenny followed me on Twitter. He saw me standing by the stage, came up and asked, 'What's up, Mo? How you keeping?'

Woah! It was a nice moment, because it's one thing him following me on social media, but to actually acknowledge me in person is another level. They say you should never meet your heroes – but Sir Lenny Henry was cool.

I was presenting the award for Best Female Performance in a Comedy Programme with the comedian Lolly Adefope and I felt as if I was looking slick! As well as my new Tom Ford blazer, I had a shirt with hidden buttons, a bowtie and tasselled loafers from Crockett & Jones. I was feeling myself!

Because of my dyslexia, I said to Lolly, 'You read out the nominations and I'll say the winner.' Because I didn't want to get it wrong and mess up somebody's big day. We went out onstage and saw a sea of people. It was pretty daunting!

I knew they'd expect me to make a joke because, well, I'm a comedian. Sometimes you've got to sing for your supper! In fact, they'd written a joke for me to say, but I rejected it. I said I'd rather either not do one or I'd make one up myself.

So, I looked out into the audience, and said, 'It's really nice to be here! It's kind of awkward that it's on TV, though, because it means I won't be able to return this nice blazer ...' It got a laugh. *Phew!*

Jessica Hynes won. When she came up, I gave her a kiss on one cheek, then went to kiss her on the other one but bottled it and pulled out halfway through. It looked kind of awkward on TV but fuck it! Nerves can do that kind of thing to you!

After we came off stage, we had to do some press and take some pictures. I didn't have to lie and pretend to be a professional footballer this time.

Later, everyone went down to the main hall where dinner was being served, but we weren't given very much. Two little guinea fowl, a carrot, some tiny potatoes. That's one thing with awards shows – they never give you enough food!

I saw a couple of people who had won BAFTAs walking around carrying them, and I felt like asking, 'Can I hold it? Just for a minute?' But I also didn't feel like doing that because I have a funny superstition about holding it.

For me, a BAFTA is like the World Cup: you don't want to touch it till you've won it because it's bad luck and it might mean that you never will hold it for real. Even when I had been handing out the award onstage, part of me had been thinking, *Oh, I don't really wanna hold it!*

• • •

After the BAFTAs ceremony had ended, we headed to the after-party, which was mad. My eyes were on stalks. I was looking all around: *Jodie Comer from* Killing Eve *just walked past me!* People seemed to be floating around. I met Jamie Redknapp, who is a really nice guy. He said, 'Yeah, I've seen some of your videos, man. Really funny!'

Wow, Jamie Redknapp's seen my videos! That's sick!

I got together at the after-party with the few Black and Asian actors also present – including Tosin, Tommy and Samson – and we all decided to get a photo together. We planned it: 'Let's meet by the stairs at eleven o'clock!' We wanted it to be like that famous Grammy picture with Will Smith, Public Enemy and Salt-N-Pepa.

The press were taking loads of photos at the BAFTAs, so the next morning, I went straight online to have a look – and saw that I *finally* got my Getty moment. Yeah, there was my picture, looking sick … but on one of them they'd called me by the wrong name.

They had called me Tommy Moutchi. And one of Tommy's pictures had *my* name by it! *Shit! Some people just can't tell Black men apart!*

• • •

The BAFTAs was the first time that I went to an official awards show after-party, but over the next couple of years, I started to go to a lot more of them. And they were always an interesting experience.

One show I went to was the GRM Daily Rated Awards. They were cool because they're mostly about Black music and I felt like I knew a lot of people there, just from being in and around the scene. Sometimes the music awards are the most fun, maybe because I feel there's less need to keep up appearances.

I got asked to host the Q Awards in 2018. That was mad just because the musicians are all megastars. People like Bono and Ed Sheeran were there. They were handing out awards to people like Noel Gallagher, Paul Weller and Nile Rodgers.

Another really good one I went to was the 2019 GQ Awards. That was wicked. Big people were there! Patrick Stewart, David Beckham, Nicole Kidman, Kylie ... and this time Hugo Boss gifted me a suit for the event.

Shit, yeah! Yes, please!

This was the first time I'd gone to an awards show on my own, without management or PR, because the night is invitation only and the guest list is so strict.

It was pretty good. The food was alright, everyone was pretty much sound and, I guess, that's because everyone was admiring how good they looked in their suits.

It was all quite laid-back. You got put on different tables and I didn't know anybody on my table. But I was sitting next to James Blunt and we had a proper chat. He's a cool guy, and really funny.

After the food, I saw Krept & Konan, which made it a bit easier for me, and made me feel like less of a Billy No-Mates: *Ah, OK, cool! Some people that I know*! Then I saw Idris Elba and Dave, the rapper. Stormzy was there as well, and I know some of his team.

It's nice when you see people from your background at awards shows and parties like that and they are just as excited as you are to be there. The feeling's quite raw because it's like, *This is a bit mad, innit?*

I bumped into one of my friends, who introduced me to some people he knew, like the head of the British Fashion Council. I was like, *Whoa!* It's mad when you start meeting people like that, who are not necessarily famous but very influential.

Then my friend asked me, 'What are you doing now?'

'Nothing,' I said.

'Good. Do you wanna come to the after-party?'

THE MAGIC WORDS! Because the after-party is what everybody wants to get to. At some awards shows, people blow off the actual awards and just head straight to the after-party. It's like the Holy Grail. Everybody wants to get in.

So, we got into a black cab and went to a street just off Primrose Hill. We got out the other side to a small, unassuming alleyway. It didn't look like much. But we walked up to the gate and were let through by the girl in charge of the guest list.

We turned around the corner, and the house that stood before us was something else. It looked like a chic 1960s mansion – in Primrose Hill! You would never know that houses like this existed, hidden away, especially in that area.

This party was sick! In front of the house was a food outlet doing free burgers and chips, and it wasn't just any old burgers and chips. They were as good as Honest Burgers! I can't remember what they were called, but they had an actual shop on Oxford Street, and they were doing the party catering!

When we got inside the house, there was a sushi buffet in the kitchen. Well, I say buffet, but it wasn't like normal where you just wander along picking up what you fancy with your fingers. They had a guy serving it up:

'What sushi would sir like?'

It was different level, man.

Konan was there and we were just chillin' and chatting when we saw Naomi Campbell walk by us. We stared at each other, and our faces said we both had the same thought:

Bloody hell! That's Naomi Campbell there!

Some of the guests were young rich kids whose dads are billionaires. I saw Brooklyn Beckham there, but I guess he's always grown up around those parties and that lifestyle, so that kind of thing is the norm for him.

As well as those rich kids, we were just seeing loads of famous faces. I was talking to Jimmy Carr and then, to my left, I saw … David Blaine. My brain went straight into an intense conversation with itself:

That's David Blaine. Should I go and talk to him?

Of course you should! Get over there!

So, I went over to him. '*Rah*, bruv! You're David Blaine, innit!'

He looked at me and gave what I guess you'd have to call an 'enigmatic' smile.

'Yeah, man,' he said. 'You wanna see The Truth?' (I don't remember if those were his exact words, but it sounds like a pretty David Blaine thing to say.)

I said, 'Yeah, go on!' But if I'm being honest with you, I was so excited, I was trying not to laugh.

Then he started showing me a sleight-of-hand magic trick.

Shit! David Blaine is showing ME a magic trick!

Loads of people crowded round to watch him perform the trick to me. It was OK but not all that special and I think I was faking my reaction a bit:

'Shit, that was amazing! That was sick!'

'Can I get a picture, please?' I asked him.

I got another of those enigmatic smiles.

'Yes, but let me show you another trick first ...'

That wasn't the wildest party I'd ever been to, but it left a real impression on me. It was one of those moments ...

•   •   •

I had loved going to those BAFTAs, even though we didn't win. Not only did they show me a glitzier side to the industry; they gave me a small insight to what success is like, and a taste of what could come. Perhaps I'd even be nominated for something else one day.

Because my own show, *The Lateish Show with Mo Gilligan*, was just about to go full steam ahead.

13

THAT MOMENT WHEN ...

You Have to Tell Jada Pinkett Smith She's Done It Wrong

*L*ooking back now, I can hardly believe how busy I was in 2018. As well as all of the tour dates, making my online videos, and doing the writing and filming for *The Big Narstie Show*, I was also working like crazy to pull my own new Channel 4 show together and make it happen.

Because I knew that this was The Big One. The one I was betting all my $25 chips on.

As soon as Syeda had told me that she was giving me the Friday night slot at ten o'clock, I had had two main reactions. The first one was very straightforward: *Oh my gosh! I've got my own TV show!*

My second reaction was rather more complex. Because I didn't feel it was just *my* show. It wasn't just for me. I wanted it, first and foremost, to be a show that working-class people could watch and feel like I was speaking to *them*. And I wanted people like me, to watch it and feel proud of the image I was portraying.

I wanted to represent my community and do it in a positive light. I didn't want to denigrate us or fall into what they call 'coonery': reinforcing and perpetuating stereotypes.

The last Black comedian to have a regularly broadcast show before me was Richard Blackwood, twenty years prior. And the last one before him was Sir Lenny Henry, fifteen years before that. I could count on one hand the number of other Black entertainers who'd had their own shows (I still can!).

I had big boots to fill and it was an incredible amount of pressure. Because in a weird way, subconsciously *and* consciously, I felt like I was representing the entire Black community.

That's how it felt to me! I didn't feel like I was representing just the Caribbean community; it was like I was representing all corners of the Black community. Not only was I speaking for young Black Britons; I had to make the older generations proud as well.

What's that famous Spider-Man quote from Uncle Ben? ('*With great power comes great responsibility.*') I knew I needed to represent myself, first and foremost, and be true to who I am. But after seeing the excitement and buzz that I received from the announcement of the show, I also knew I didn't want to let anyone down.

The time slot made me feel even more pressure. *Ten o'clock on a Friday*. You just need to look at who else has chat shows in that slot: Jonathan Ross and Graham Norton. The two BIGGEST chat show hosts that this country has produced in the past twenty years, and there I was, up against their shows.

Let me put it in football terms. It's like Jonathan Ross and Graham Norton are Man City and Liverpool in the Premier League, and there's me turning up as Brentford F.C. A plucky underdog. In fact, getting that show and that timeslot has given me a whole new affinity for Brentford F.C.!

How funny is that?! From knowing nothing about them, I now know that Brentford are a good young team, with a slick new stadium next to Kew Bridge, and have just been promoted to the Premier League. Suddenly, I want that team to do well! I feel like they're representing me!

•   •   •

The 'first task', as Syeda had said, was to choose a production company. I was still very new to the world of TV and still didn't really know how it worked, so I was just going along to meetings to see what happened.

Sometimes, those companies made the first move themselves! When I joined *The Big Narstie Show*, I went to a first meeting with their production company, Expectation, at their swanky office in Notting Hill. I was there to talk about *The Big Narstie Show*: I didn't say a word about getting my own show. But Ben Wicks, their executive producer, just came right out and said:

'We've heard you've got your own show as well, Mo, and we'd love to work on that.'

What?

I was gobsmacked and Ben just laughed; the television industry has a very good grapevine. There is always someone in TV who talks to someone else. People always know your news, somehow.

But I just carried on trying to keep my cards close to my chest. 'You never know,' I told Ben. 'Let's see if it happens.'

I met with a few other production companies as well. They were all pitching their ideas to me of what they could do for my show. I did a lot of listening and a lot of thinking, because I had some strong ideas myself for what I wanted to do.

I had started off thinking the show would follow a high-grade sketch show/chat show format. But as I picked up more experience on *The Big Narstie Show*, I knew that I wanted to go full chat show with *some* sketches, games and audience interaction.

I knew Expectation knew how to do shows like that, so I went with them. I just figured, *OK, cool, I can really trust you guys on this.* And then I started working like crazy to get it right.

We started off with some seriously long writing days. I had a little team of writers around me and we began working on ideas, sketches, scripts and games to play on the show. And I realised that writing for the ten o'clock slot is a little different from writing for eleven o'clock.

There are more restrictions on what you can do and say. We couldn't be a full-on, anything-goes anarchic type thing, which was exactly what the *The Big Narstie Show* was and still is. For example, I was used to wearing hoodies and jeans on there, but we toyed around with the idea that I was gonna wear suits on my own show.

I must admit, I didn't like the idea at first. We had a bit of back and forth on it, but in the end, I said, 'OK, let's do it. Let's try wearing suits.' Because, in my heart, I preferred the idea and knew it would help in differentiating my show from the work I'd done on *The Big Narstie Show*.

As well as writing material, we were trying to book guests for interview. This could be quite a hard task. Some people couldn't do it because they were genuinely busy, but I think a few others were like, 'Mo Gilligan – who is he? I don't really know this guy – why should I do his show?'

For the same reason, Channel 4 decided to launch the show in the summer of 2019. Fewer people watch TV in the summer because they're off on holidays, but I feel like it's a good time to do a soft launch of a show by an up-and-coming guy like myself. You're kind of up against it if you launch a show around Christmastime and you're battling against *Love Actually* and *Home Alone* for solid, we're-gonna-renew-your-show ratings.

It might sound crazy to people who aren't in TV – and, in a way, it *is* – but we worked for two years to get the format of *The Lateish Show* right. *Two years!* The next step was making sure that everyone knew about it.

I spent the two or three weeks leading up to the first show doing as much promo as I could. Any TV show or radio show or newspaper that would have me, I was there. It was a weird time – interviewers were telling me they were excited for me, but I wasn't all that sure whether all of them *really* knew who I was.

I was excited to go into Virgin Radio and talk to Chris Evans on his breakfast show. I had loved his shows as a kid, like *TFI Friday* and *Don't Forget Your Toothbrush*, and they were definitely some of the blueprints I had for *The Lateish Show*. I wanted my show to feel as fun as those had.

I was honest with Chris in the interview. I said to him, 'Look, your shows have definitely given me ideas and inspiration. I want to emulate what you did but give it my own flavour.'

Chris was great about it. 'I've seen a clip of your show and it looks really good, Mo,' he said. 'I wish you the best and I think you've got a bright future.' Chris Evans didn't need to say that, but it was great that he did. I felt like I had been given his blessing.

The first episode of *The Lateish Show* was televised on 19 July 2019, and we threw absolutely everything at it. First impressions are so important, so we had some serious big-name guests on the first show: Tyson Fury, Steve Coogan and Asim Chaudhry.

Jessie J was on as well and she knocked it out of the park when it came to one of our games. We had a game called 'Nursery Grimes' where our guests had to sing the words of a classic nursery rhyme to the tune of a famous pop track.

'If it's "Pony", I'm leaving!' Jessie said. But when she got given 'Old MacDonald Had a Farm' and Whitney Houston's 'I Will Always Love You' she threw herself into it. Looking well glam in a sharp green strap-dress, she gave it loads of Whitney tremors and vibrato as she belted out those poignant, moving words ...

'Old MacDonald had a farm,
(E-I-E-I-I-O)
And on his farm, he had a cow,
(E-I-E-I-E-O)'

And then that big, shoulder-heaving chorus:

'With a moo, moo here ...'

When the show went out, I just sat and watched it with my family. It was a proper moment. I didn't know what to say. I was just thinking, *Oh my gosh, that's fully me on the TV! With my own show! I've actually done it!* It was something I will never forget.

It felt great, but at the same time I couldn't dwell on it and take it in too much because I was already thinking what we were going to do for the following week's show. And the following week. And the following week. There was no time really to process what was happening.

It was true of the whole series. As soon as an episode had aired, I'd be thinking, *Bang! It's time for the next one!* I was mentally taking notes as I watched the shows: *What do we need to do differently?* It wasn't till the series had finished that I could sit back, watch them and actually enjoy them.

Channel 4 liked the first show and told me that more than a million people had seen it, which they were happy with. Then there were more viewers watching it on catch-up and online. And the other good sign was the number of people who wanted to come to the live recordings.

The studio for *The Lateish Show* held six hundred audience members. In no time, we were getting nearly twice as many as that turning up, hoping to see the show recorded. We were having to turn away more than five hundred people at the door. One night we actually had to turn away a thousand.

People were driving down from Birmingham, and all sorts. It was cool, because recordings can drag on and get *long*. It was unfortunate we had to turn people away, but good that we were recording at Television Centre in White City, because at least the people who didn't get in could go to Westfield and grab themselves a cheeky Nando's.

The long queues and the pandemonium on the door helped us, though. It made us seem like the show everyone wanted to be at. Soon, we were getting calls from Sony Music and the like: 'Yeah, is that *The Lateish Show*? If you want any of our artists on your show, just let us know …'

Mel B was on the second show and we'd asked fans who their favourite Spice Girl was. They didn't know she was standing right behind them – man, their faces when they turned around and saw her were hilarious!

Mel and I also stood back to back and banged out M-Beat and General Levy's 'Incredible', you know the one – 'Wicked, wicked, jungle is massive' – which felt pretty surreal to me. After the show, she invited me down to a Spice Girls reunion launch event. I was like, 'Me? Really? Are you sure? Gosh, I would love to … I *grew up* with the Spice Girls!'

Shaggy was also on another episode of the show and I wanted to do a sketch with him called 'Mind Your Business', with me as the geezer character. We were recording the song for it on a Monday, and I wrote the lyrics on the night before.

When I met Shaggy in the recording studio, I had a feeling he didn't have a clue who I was, what I do or even why he was there. But I didn't mind that at all. He was a lovely guy, and my only concern was, *Right, I've got to get this song with Shaggy!*

We started recording the song and I was doing the first verse in character as the geezer character but kept fucking it up. I kept saying the words that I'd written down wrong. After about the third time, I said, 'OK, I'm ready! This is the proper one now!'

'Are you *sure* you're ready?' Shaggy grinned. 'Are you *sure* you know the words?'

'No, no, I was just messing around before,' I said. 'This is the real one.' I was totally blagging it!

Luckily, that time it went proper smooth. We recorded the song and filmed a video for it, with Shaun Williamson, who played Barry from *EastEnders*, in it. I still do a double take whenever I think about it now: *I brought Barry from* EastEnders *and Shaggy together!*

We did a great sketch with Danny Dyer involving a virtual-assistant device, like Alexa, that we named 'The Danny'. We had a prototype made for it of a speaker with a big hand on top, giving the finger. I'd ask it questions, and Danny's angry voice would blare back to me:

'Danny, what's the weather like outside?'

'How the fuck am I supposed to know? Why don't you look out the fuckin' window, you mug?'

I remembered, as a kid, buying pirate DVDs of Danny in stuff like *Football Factory* … and now here he was, sitting having a laugh with me!

It was one of the best things about the first series of *The Lateish Show*. Yes, it was work, and I wanted to make sure the best show possible every week – but also, I was meeting some amazing people and some heroes. And that was never truer than when Jada Pinkett Smith came on.

I knew that we'd booked Jada, but I never quite believed she would come. Before the show, every bit of me was thinking, *Mmm,*

I bet she doesn't show up! She's PROPER Hollywood royalty and she's in some of my favourite ever films, like *Menace II Society* and *The Nutty Professor*. She's a full-on megastar!

We had a strong show even if Jada didn't turn up. We had Aisling Bea; my main man and New York dining companion, David Schwimmer; and Ricky Wilson from Kaiser Chiefs. Ricky performed a song ... and then I introduced Jada Pinkett Smith to the audience as she walked out onto the interview stage.

The studio audience lost their minds, because they'd had no idea she was going to be on! They all jumped up out of their seats and started clapping wildly. You'd have thought the president had walked out! (Well, Obama, maybe. Probably not Trump.)

Jada sat down and I interviewed her. Like Shaggy, she clearly hadn't got the first idea who I was, but we had a great chat. She talked about posting a video online of her dancing to her son Jaden's track: 'I thought he might think it was embarrassing but he liked it, so that was cool!'

I roped Jada into our usual dance-off game at the end of the show. We divided the studio audience into two halves, blue and green, and chose a guy from each team to do the dance-off. Each person in the winning team gets a bag of electronic goodies so everybody is always bang up for it.

Jada had to choose the winner. The two young guys took it in turns to gyrate and bust some moves in front of her. 'OK! Which is it, Jada – blue, or green?' I asked her and passed her the mic.

'Oh, I really don't know.' She smiled. 'You know what I'm going to do, Mo? I'm going to call it a draw!'

Huh? A draw? We only had about three hundred bags of gadgets to give out – we didn't have enough for everyone! I then had the producer in my ear:

'Mo! You're going to have to get Jada to pick a winner ...'

Gulp!

The floor manager called, 'Cut!' and I said, 'Jada, I'm really sorry, but you need to actually choose a winner!' She flashed a huge smile: 'Oh, OK!'

We rolled the cameras again and Jada picked the green team. And I went home that night thinking, *I just told Jada Pinkett Smith that she got it wrong!* It made me laugh, imagining her on the phone to Will, moaning about the UK comedian who made her do another take on his silly TV show. But I doubt she would. She's one of the nicest celebrities I've ever met.

Another guest I had on who was the man of the moment in the summer of 2019 was Ovie Soko from *Love Island*, who was a surprise guest on 'Nursery Grimes', with Eamonn Holmes, Dermot O'Leary and the late Caroline Flack. Ovie sang 'The Wheels on the Bus' to the tune of 'Return of the Mack'. It was ... memorable.

That was what the first series of *The Lateish Show* was like. *Memorable*. It was full of crazy moments. It was non-stop and a million miles per hour as we were making it. Then, when it was finished, I caught my breath and thought to myself, *Man! Did all that really happen?* It's like going on a roller coaster. You only realise how crazy it is when you step off and are a bit dizzy.

Sometimes people ask me what the best moment in my career has been so far. There've been a few, but having my own show is right up there, because once it had aired, nobody could take it away from me. I felt like if I died there and then, I'd die a happy man.

I'd done my own show and I had got to do it my own way – you know what? I don't think many people get to do that, especially for their first show.

The Lateish Show had given me a truly amazing career highlight … and I was about to enjoy another one, which was absolutely mind-boggling.

I was about to drop a Netflix special.

14

THAT MOMENT WHEN ...

*You Call Your
Mum a Dickhead on
a Netflix Special*

Weirdly, I'd recorded my Netflix special while I was working on *The Lateish Show*. It was around the time when so much was going on in my life that it was crazy – it still is! – but doing the Netflix thing felt proper, proper special.

Why? Well, just let me explain …

When I was growing up, a lot of the comedians that I looked up to were American comics like Eddie Murphy. I loved his films! And, as I got older, I paid extra-special attention to his stand-up specials, like *Delirious* and *Raw*. And now here I was, on the brink of my own televised special.

When Polly first told me that Netflix had got in touch, I couldn't take it in. It wasn't only that the idea of doing a special was so exciting; I was also going to be on the same platform as greats such as Dave Chappelle and Chris Rock.

A special should be like an album: every bit of material has a place and a reason as to why it's been written in. It's got to be cohesive.

For *The Coupla Cans Tour* I'd condensed almost ten years of work into an hour-and-twenty-minute routine. It had sort of been my first album – and now, I thought that the Netflix special could be the deluxe version of that album.

•   •   •

When Netflix had first got in touch with Polly about the possibility of a special, it was exciting but I knew that I couldn't get too carried away.

I figured they probably asked loads of comics to send them stuff and there was no guarantee that they would like what I did, or what we sent them. When it came down to it, I knew that, as far as Netflix were concerned, I was a very small fish in a huge ocean.

Polly, Geli and I put the test special together from a few of my *Coupla Cans* gigs, called it *Momentum*, and sent it on to Netflix. Fingers crossed! Just before Christmas 2018, Polly called me to tell me that they loved it.

She said that their producers had also had more to say:

'We feel that it could be bigger,' they said.

'We want to reshoot it and make it available worldwide.'

We had started out with the plan that the special would be a limited release, but now they wanted to turn it into a Netflix Original and stream it to 190 countries.

Wow!

The fact that the biggest streaming platform in the world had said they wanted to make the show *bigger* indicated that they were serious about it.

When I got the big thumbs up from Netflix, I was well excited, but I also knew that I had some serious work ahead. It brought back the same feelings I'd had when I started out on the Sunday Show, only on a much, much grander scale.

I knew I'd need to stand out from the crowd somehow because there are so many great comics on that platform. What could I, a Black British comedian, do to make my comedy relatable to the guy in Arkansas, or the woman in Bolivia?

Well, one starting point was that one of the key ingredients of my material is music. I've always been surrounded by music, and I love using it on stage, because I think it helps bring the show to life, and my audience can relate to it.

Initially, I had the idea of using a loop pedal while I was performing – proper Ed Sheeran stuff! It sounded sick, but I knew it would be hard to implement, particularly because different countries' copyright laws prevented us from playing some of the songs I wanted to include. So, I hit on a plan B: *why not use original, newly composed music, and do it with a live band?*

As soon as I thought of it, I was totally into the idea. I loved the thought of having musicians up there onstage with me, like I was an old-school showman.

I asked my old school friends Louis and Mark to help me with the music. Louis composed the score, and Mark, who knows loads of musicians, organised the arrangements. They did a great job. When we did the first rehearsal, it was sounding good, but I told the band to make sure they were enjoying playing the music. Because I wanted them to sound *relaxed*.

'It's got to sound really smooth. Tropicana, no bits,' I told them. 'Not like you're just reading the notes.' I explained I wanted them to sort of freestyle and express themselves. I wanted it to be collaborative. It would mean we were a team.

When we all got together for the first rehearsal, we started off with my Rastafarian nursery rhymes routine. The first time we ran through it together, it sounded good, but by the second attempt everyone had loosened up and it sounded amazing! *That* was the moment when I realised that the whole Netflix show was going to be sick.

I did a couple of warm-up shows with the live band and I could feel it was really coming together. It felt natural, and I could tell that the audience thought it was a little bit different to other comedy shows they'd seen. Which was exactly what I wanted!

• • •

We filmed the actual Netflix special at the Hackney Empire in April 2019. I didn't know you had to film two versions when you record a special, in order to get close-ups and shots from multiple angles, so I had to perform two shows in one day. The night before, I was pretty anxious, which doesn't normally happen to me. I don't usually get nerves the day before. But I just felt aware of the magnitude of what I was about to do, and I started overthinking every aspect of it.

That feeling persisted when I turned up on the afternoon of the first show and saw the vast army of cameramen, lighting technicians and stagehands getting into place. I gawped at them all, getting ready for this major production, and I couldn't help but think, *Wow, all of this for* my *show?*

My own production company, Momo G, co-produced the special and I acted as an executive producer, which was a massive deal. Before everyone took their places, we had a meeting – me, the director and the head of each department. I wasn't sure what to say. I was in awe of everyone working on the show and grateful they were on board. I just wanted to tell everyone to do what they do best: I mean, what was *I* supposed to say to the director? 'Keep directing'?

Filming a big thing like a special makes you realise how many people are involved. You have everyone telling you 'Good luck!' and even if you already think it's going to go great, other people's nervous energy can be contagious.

I normally try to take a quiet moment before I step onstage. Left on my own, I'm quite calm and I can just go out there to perform. But, right now, I was very much not on my own …

• • •

When I walked out onstage for the first show of the Netflix recording, and the audience were all screaming, it felt weird. It was almost like an out-of-body experience. Initially, it didn't feel natural because I was still overthinking everything. If you go back and watch that moment, you can see in my eyes that I'm mesmerized.

I was thinking about the cameras – *Where are they? Which one should I be talking down the barrel of?* I felt super-conscious of my footing, like I'd forgotten my normal walk. *Do I look like a duck onstage? Or do I look like a pigeon?* I was crazy nervous for, oh, ten seconds – but then, thankfully, it passed.

And I went into show mode.

Because, despite the strangeness and the pressure of that particular night, I was still basically doing exactly what I'd done hundreds of times before, and what I'd done the last eighteen months on my first tour. I was walking out to do a live stand-up show. Everything I'd worked for over the last ten years had built up to this moment.

It's a funny thing because musicians always get their big entrances, but comedians never really do. Beyoncé can just step onstage and stand there for a few minutes, the wind machine blowing in her hair, while everyone screams her name. You don't really get that in comedy, but I wish you did!

Even so, I love the feeling when you first walk out to entertain a comedy crowd. With a live band with you, like I had there in Hackney, it is the best feeling in the world.

I wanted to perform the show and make it look effortless, almost as if I had been filming TV specials for years. I had tried to make the material timeless, so that people could watch it in five or ten years' time and it would still feel current and funny.

I wanted people to watch it in other countries and get a great first impression of my comedy.

I went out to a blare of cool music from the live band. After that initial bout of nervousness, I took to it like a duck to water. I quickly forgot we were even recording a Netflix special.

I started off the show with some tried-and-tested material about how all mums are dickheads. I had a routine about how mums would make you put back expensive things in the super-market because they couldn't afford it. I would joke about my own mum in my shows. In fact, within the first two minutes of my special, I had done an impression of my younger self in a sulk with her at the shops, shuffling off and saying under my breath, 'Oh shut up with your fat ankles.'

I've had people who have seen me live, and heard me doing my all mums are dickheads routine, who have said to me:

'Woah, Mo! Does your mum know about those jokes?'

And the answer is – *of course*! I love her to bits. She knows that, and she knows I don't really mean the stuff that I say onstage. I don't have to ask her, 'Mum, do you mind if I do a joke about your ankles?' We have got a great understanding about it – and about *everything*.

Mum is well proud of me and comes to see me perform whenever she can. If she could be in a front-row seat for every single show that I do, she would be! And she was right there in the Hackney Empire for that first Netflix recording.

In fact, Mum is very happy about being featured in my act. All my family have a great sense of humour, and we know when we take the piss out of each other it's all good-natured fun.

The first recording of the show, in the afternoon, went great. I was in my element. And to top that, I'd enjoyed myself, which I think translates on-screen. I was playing to the cameras but also it was all about the audience. And it worked.

Now the first half was done, I felt like I'd cycled to the top of a very tall hill, and could look forward to the easy ride down.

The second recording went even better. I was just vibing and having a lot of fun. The cool thing about it was that at both shows, the crowds didn't know it was being recorded for Netflix.

They just thought they were coming along to a normal stand-up gig, which was cool as it meant that I knew the crowd were there just to support me, and I think it made for a better night, where everyone was just living in the moment.

• • •

My Netflix special went live across the world at eight o'clock in the morning UK time on 30 September 2019. By the time I woke up at nine o'clock my phone was going completely crazy. That day was so mad and a little overwhelming. I'd never had a day like it before. Previously, I'd had people congratulating me for *The Big Narstie Show* and *The Lateish Show*, but *nothing* prepares you for when you drop a Netflix special.

The feedback was nuts. I had people messaging me from all over the world, from the guy down the street in London to people in far-flung places like Brazil and Indonesia. After about six months, it started to ease up a bit, but still to this day I'll have people tagging me in posts or tweeting me because they've just watched it.

Even now, I can still hardly believe that I've done it. To get that opportunity to put myself out there to the world – it's mind-blowing. There's not even a single thing that I'd do differently. I'll never forget the day that it came out and I eagerly typed in my name on Netflix. When the image for *Momentum* flashed up, I couldn't believe it!

Overall, I was so overwhelmed by the response to the Netflix special that I had to get away from social media for a bit. It was just too full-on. Twitter, Instagram and Facebook were nuts. It all becomes a bit crazy, and I can see how it gets to people. It can get in your head – both the positive *and* the negative.

After the special came out, I went to LA and everyone I met out there told me that they loved it. They all thought it was amazing. I almost wondered if they were lying, because the moment was so surreal. Me, the boy from south London, being told that I'm a winner in Hollywood!

Ultimately, doing a special is what comedy is all about. I was given the opportunity to make people from 190 different countries laugh! It was a powerful and humbling experience that I'll always be grateful for.

In fact, for a comic, it's hard to think of anything that tops doing a Netflix special.

Well, except, maybe, winning a BAFTA …

15

THAT MOMENT WHEN ...

You Win a BAFTA with Sweaty Toes

*L*ess than a year after my Netflix special had come out, I got nominated for a BAFTA for *The Lateish Show*. I found that I'd been nominated in the June of 2020, but the story starts long before that …

A few years prior, my girlfriend had been reading a lot about the law of attraction: the idea that negative thinking attracts negative experiences, while positive thoughts lead to more attractive outcomes. And one Christmas she gave me a box, all wrapped up in Christmas paper.

'This is a law-of-attraction box,' she said.

Huh? I ripped open the paper and looked in the box. It contained three pictures: one of a house, one of a dream car and one of a BAFTA.

It was a really touching gift because after that, my outlook on life started to change in so many ways. The law of attraction came into my life at the perfect time. It made me more positive and helped me enjoy life in the here and now, while still thinking ahead to what I wanted to achieve. Prior to that, I hadn't given thought to any awards I might win. They weren't the reason I got into comedy. But from the moment I looked in that box, I started daring to dream.

If I can get a bit sincere here – my career in comedy is all about the years of blood, sweat and tears that have led me to where I am today. It's all about creating something that a lot of people love and making art that speaks to something bigger than just yourself while bringing people joy.

Yeah. *That's* what it's all about.

So, even after our nomination for *The Big Narstie Show*, I didn't fully grasp how prestigious a BAFTA was, or what winning one meant. If I ever thought about BAFTAs, which was not very often, I pictured the big movie awards when a few Hollywood celebrities come to London for the night.

I was pretty clueless, really, I had seen the NTAs on TV before, but that was about it. However, as I got more and more into the TV world and started to understand the importance associated with some of these awards, I fully realised the importance of the BAFTAs.

And then I did the weirdest thing, man. In the May, weeks before I got nominated, while I was chilling on the sofa at home, I wrote an acceptance speech for winning a BAFTA.

Fuck knows what I was thinking of! I hadn't even got the slightest clue that I was about to be nominated. I don't know what came over me. Maybe that angel and devil were on my shoulders again, both of them whispering, 'It's time to write your BAFTA speech!

So, I did. I wrote a BAFTA acceptance speech in the 'Notes' app on my phone. It was even more mad as the COVID-19 pandemic had affected everything by now, all events had been cancelled, and

I was locked down at home just like everybody else. *Will there even be a BAFTAs this year?* I thought.

Well, yes, as I found out three weeks later, there would be. After I woke up from a beautiful lie-in to find my phone was blowing up with everyone hitting me up with congratulations. Everything was pinging off and I was getting text after text saying, 'Well done, bruv!'

Huh? What's going on?

I looked at my Twitter and it was the same thing: lots of people saying, 'Congratulations to my guy Mo!' I was still thinking, *For what?* Then I looked at the messages properly and the penny dropped:

Oh, shit, I got nominated for a BAFTA!

I. Was. Buzzing! Absolutely buzzing! *Oh my gosh! I got nominated for a BAFTA!* It felt proper, proper nuts. I felt like I was still dreaming.

In that moment, I was just so happy to get nominated, I wasn't even thinking about whether I might win or not. I was just so happy that I had got nominated for the first series of my own show. It was a lot to take in.

I was also happy because it was for me and for everyone else that had worked on the show. There were people that would stay till midnight to work on scripts because things often changed at the last minute.

When a boxer wins a title, it isn't just their win. It's their team's win: the family, and friends, and everyone who gave up time and believed in the dream. All of those long hours in the gym, away from the family just for that one moment. Everybody has made sacrifices. They should all share the glory. When you win, everyone around you wins.

I was nominated in the BAFTA category for Best Entertainment Performance. The full list of nominees was:

- Frankie Boyle for *Frankie Boyle's New World Order*
- Mo Gilligan for *The Lateish Show ... with Mo Gilligan*
- Lee Mack for *Would I Lie to You?*
- Graham Norton for *The Graham Norton Show*

OK – these were some major guys that I was among here! I was in the presence of some exceptional comedians, who were all well established in the industry and I had no expectations of winning, but after the buzz of the nomination had died down, I realised my chances, one in four, really weren't bad.

The law of attraction says that you have to put positive energy out into the world to receive positive things. So, I wrote a note and I stuck it on my TV cabinet at home. The note said: *RESERVED FOR BAFTA 31/7/20.*

I still have that note.

Man, it was weird! After I got nominated, every night I was going to sleep imagining what it would be like to win the BAFTA. Normally, when I go to bed, I say my positive affirmations then drift off to sleep.

That's my routine, but now, suddenly, every night, I was thinking about what it would be like winning the BAFTA. Thinking about saying my speech to an audience: who I'm gonna thank, and how I'm gonna do it, how it would feel and even what I would wear.

The BAFTAs were going to be recorded on Friday 31 July, and then would be broadcast on TV later that day. On the night before the ceremony, as I went to brush my teeth before bed, I suddenly said this to myself in the mirror:

'This time tomorrow night, I'm gonna be a BAFTA winner!'

I remember that I said it exactly like that. I didn't say that I *might* be a BAFTA winner: I said that I *will* be. I don't know why, but I just had a really good feeling about it.

Of course, like everything else in 2020, the awards were unusual because they had to be held online due to the pandemic. They were doing them via Zoom, which meant there was no red carpet and none of the usual grandeur expected at awards ceremonies.

This didn't stop me being excited and, in fact, I didn't mind it. It's nice to be at the big star-studded events, but when I really thought hard about it, I figured, *You know what? I'd rather spend the time with my loved ones. That's what I really wanna do.*

So, on the evening of the awards, my girlfriend and I were cooking for hours. We cooked chicken and mac 'n' cheese and got the house ready. I found a white shirt to wear. I had to do a little online rehearsal at one o'clock that afternoon, because the show was being recorded in a studio, with all the guests and nominees appearing on links via Zoom.

Then it came to 2.45pm. Showtime.

OK, let's roll!

I was sitting at the table in my front room. I had my computer in front of me and my phone propped up with my speech ready in the Notes app. If I won, the last thing I wanted was to have to go scrambling around the room looking for my phone!

I felt confident but the closer it got, the more my nerves were building.

Just before the show began, I went into Photos on my phone, and scrolled to pictures from a few years back when I was still working in retail. I looked through them and thought to myself: *Yeah, I remember that! And that! That's where I've come from!* It made me realise the journey I'd been on.

Originally, I hadn't planned on dressing up, as I was in the comfort of my own home, but then I thought if do end up winning this, I want to look smart. So, I'd compromised with the smart white shirt ... and shorts on my bottom half. It was my version of smart casual: the shirt was smart; the shorts were casual! Most people working from home can probably relate when they're on these video calls all day, right?

I remember that my feet were sweaty. You know when you're anxious and you get clammy? My feet felt really sweaty between my toes as I sat there, nervously, with just my laptop and my phone.

Then a producer from the BAFTAs appeared on my screen and told me that the show was about to start. Cool! I closed Photos and opened up Notes. *Just in case ...*

After a few minutes, they let me into this big digital awards room. There must have been thirty or forty people there: *loads* of talent. It was everyone who had been nominated for the first three awards. I spotted Graham Norton, Jodie Comer and Phoebe Waller-Bridge, just to name a few.

Everyone started talking and joking around: 'How you doing? How's everyone? *Rah*, this is fun, guys! You alright?' To be honest, I was just trying hard to see what everybody's houses were like in the backgrounds! I love *Homes Under the Hammer*, so getting to see inside the houses of all this talent was mad.

So, we were all chatting away, and then a producer told us, 'OK, guys, we're gonna do the first awards!' The show began with Richard Ayoade hosting ... and we were the very first award up! The same as when we'd been nominated the year before!

Shit – I hope that's not a bad omen!

Then Paul Mescal and Daisy Edgar Jones from *Normal People* came on-screen to present the award:

OK! Here we go!

I nervously took a deep breath. My toes were still sweating.

They ran the VT packages of all the nominees: Graham Norton flashed on the screen, following by Lee Mack, then Frankie Boyle and then, finally, they showed me.

After this, they headed back to the studio where Paul and Daisy were preparing to announce the winner.

I was actually feeling OK, pretty cool: *Right, this is it! This is the moment!*

They open up the envelope and then suddenly my name flashes up on the studio screen: *THE LATEISH SHOW WITH MO GILLIGAN.*

Huh? What was happening? I was confused. It just didn't register. I went into shock. For a few seconds, I didn't know what was happening and suddenly I had appeared on the main screen where they were saying my name:

'And the winner is ... *The Lateish Show with Mo Gilligan!*'

It wasn't till they actually said my name that it felt real. *Woah!* The moment when they say your name is insane! I'd felt like I might win, but I wasn't prepared for them ACTUALLY SAYING MY NAME! A million things were suddenly going around my head at once:

I've done it! I've actually won a BAFTA!

The thing with me is, when I'm shocked, I mean *happy shocked*, I talk a lot. I laugh, and I talk a lot. I remember one year getting surprised with a birthday party, and I just kept laughing all night. I couldn't fathom what was going on and I laughed and laughed and laughed.

Well, this was like that, times a hundred.

At special moments like this ... *you need to just live life.* I knew that I should probably compose myself and try to act cool. But I also knew something else: *There is no way I can compose myself and try to act cool!*

So, I didn't even try. I was so excited that I was just all over the place!

'Oh my God,' I said. 'I was *not* prepared for this!' I was laughing my head off. 'I wrote a speech. This is an incredible honour!'

I glanced down at my phone, still laughing.

'I want to thank my girlfriend, my close friends, my family ...' then I thanked the people at Channel 4 and at Expectation. But I had more to say. Important stuff ...

'On a personal note, this award means so much to me. I can't tell you! Even the names I'm with blew my mind away to be here ... it also gives hope to so many people who look like me, sound like me and are from the same background as me ... UTC – we brought it home, bruv! We brought it home! Thank you! Oh my gosh! I'm so gassed!'

I collapsed back into gales of laughter as the producers cut away from me and back to the studio. Richard Ayoade smiled. 'Congratulations to Mo – not prepared, but he wrote a speech!' he noted, dryly, which made me laugh even more.

My girlfriend had been in the bedroom and could hear what was going on. I had heard her say, *'What?!'* when I won, and as soon as they cut back to the studio, she came running out. She was crying, and we were both jumping around the room for joy.

Yeah, I was jumping for joy – in my smart shirt, and my shorts, and my feet that were sweating between the toes!

As I signed out of the celebrity-filled Zoom room, Graham Norton and Lee Mack both said, 'Congratulations, well done!', which was nice of them. Then there was a producer on the line, telling me that I had to go and do some press for the BAFTAs post-awards interviews.

'Remember, it's confidential that you've won, so don't tell anyone, OK?' he said. Because the show wasn't being broadcast till the evening, they didn't want anyone knowing in advance.

So, I did the press interviews afterwards, where journalists were asking me questions like: 'Hey Mo, how do you feel about it? You've just won!'

I answered them ... but I just didn't know what to do with myself. I was telling them, 'I feel amazing! I didn't know it was gonna happen, bro!' And I kept saying, literally out loud:

'Oh my God! I just won a BAFTA! That. Is. Mad!'

When the interviews had finished, I had some time to kill before the awards show was aired later that evening and I wasn't able to tell anyone that I'd won. I didn't know what to do with myself, so I just went for a drive and grabbed some ice cream. I had no idea what else to do.

Lots of people have said to me, 'Ah, you know, it would have been better if you were actually at the event!' But I got to experience that for the first time the year before when we were nominated for *The Big Narstie Show* and I wore my Tom Ford suit. This time I actually won it and then got to celebrate with the people I loved. The way I thought about it was this:

This year I was supposed to embark on a world tour but then the pandemic happened and all my work has been cancelled.

I wasn't sure what was going to happen. So, if you'd told me then that I'd end up winning my first BAFTA for my debut show, in the comfort of my own home, I'd say that's not a bad result. Being with my girlfriend just felt special because in that year all we'd had was each other, so to be with each other in that moment was the icing on the cake.

I knew I wasn't supposed to tell anybody I had won till the TV show had aired but I told Polly and Geli. I could hear Polly crying on the phone. It meant so much to her – almost as much as it did to me. Because they had been there almost from the start.

But I didn't tell anybody else. I was hardly gonna go on social media and tell everybody! In fact, I went on my socials and posted this:

'Guys, wish me luck! It's the big BAFTAs today!'

I did the same thing in my lads' WhatsApp group chat. I wasn't trying to cheat them: it was the exact opposite. I wanted the people closest to me to enjoy my victory in the moment, just like I had. I didn't want to spoil it for them.

●　●　●

Later that night, when the BAFTAs were being shown on telly, I got my family around to watch it with me (they had just started to relax the lockdown a little, so I was allowed to do that, before you snitches out there get any ideas!). No one had any idea that I had won.

My family arrived just in time for the show and I put the TV on and told them, 'OK, guys, it's starting. I'm up for the first award!' I sat them down and watched their faces closely as I came up on the VT package. They all cheered.

I sneakily got my phone out to record their reaction and then my name was announced: 'THE WINNER IS MO GILLIGAN FOR *THE LATEISH SHOW WITH MO GILLIGAN*.'

Man, they were going mad! All jumping around the room, like me and my girlfriend had been earlier in the day! I was trying to shush them so they could hear my speech, because I had bigged them up in it ... but they were just too excited and missed it!

I couldn't blame them – because so was I. Watching it on TV was just as exciting as winning the award earlier in the day. Maybe even more so.

And one reason winning the BAFTA meant so much to me was that it shows people from my community that we *can* win awards and *we can do it our way*. It was just like when I first got given the show on Channel 4. It felt like I was representing my people.

· · ·

As soon as my win had been officially announced, I had to do a few more press interviews. I talked to the news outlets, then, when that had finished, it was time for mac 'n' cheese, wings, pizza and a good chill with the family, followed by loads of alcohol.

At one point, I stepped outside, just to get some air and have a little think. A neighbour just so happened to be out on his balcony as well, and shouted over.

'Mo, I heard you won a BAFTA! Congratulations!'

'Thanks a lot, man!'

I had just won the biggest award that you can win in British TV. And I celebrated it how I wanted to, with my family and loved ones. Life just can't get any better than that, right?

Wrong! Because the next day, my team, Arsenal, only went and won the FA Cup!

I've done the double – the BAFTA and my team won the FA Cup!

My phone didn't stop all weekend, I had messages of congratulations from friends in TV to people I used to go to school with. The news even travelled to St Lucia, where my dad was now living, and he sent me a lovely message to congratulate me.

I knew that winning the BAFTA was great, but it wasn't the end goal. It wasn't the destination. I wasn't going to start resting on my laurels.

Now I'd had a taste of it, it felt like anything was possible: *bring on the Emmy, the Golden Globe, the Oscar, I'll even go for the Nobel Peace Prize!*

I don't tend to dwell on my wins too much. I'll celebrate and take stock, but then it's on to the next thing.

Because as the great Nipsey Hu$$le used to say: *The Marathon Continues …*

16

THAT MOMENT WHEN ...

You Shine The Spotlight on Others

MO_2

Not long after I won my BAFTA, I woke up one morning and thought, *What's next?*

I'd managed to do a lot of things in a short space of time: get my own TV show, shoot a Netflix special, travel all over the world, win a BAFTA. That's the thing with winning awards, or with any kind of career achievement, really. You have to keep driving forwards. Keep striving. It's too easy to get complacent and let your creative energy dip. I don't want that to happen.

I want to be like sports people I admire, like Serena Williams, LeBron James and Lewis Hamilton. They are just singular in their quest for greatness. They've never rested when they've succeeded: they've kept going and are always thinking, *What's next?*

It's like, when you've climbed Mount Snowdon, do you stop there? No. You've got to tackle Everest. Life doesn't stop, and there is always a new challenge. Whenever LeBron posts on Instagram, he uses the hashtag *#StriveForGreatness*. I love that.

There are so many things that I still want to achieve in my career, but the important point for me to remember is that it's not all about me. When I started making *The Lateish Show*, I was intent on representing my community on television, and that's still how I see things. In fact, now I've had a bit of success, it's truer than ever.

The way I see it is, when the spotlight is shining on me right now, it's important for me to shine it on others – and that is why I made the documentary *Black, British and Funny*. Which had been a very long time coming ...

• • •

I had the idea quite a while ago of making a documentary about how difficult Black comedians have traditionally found it to break out in the UK. In fact, I'd first pitched the concept for it three or four years back.

I'd been into Vice TV for a meeting and explained the idea. In that sort of place, you always get the older cool guy hanging out with the young hipsters, and the geezer I talked to was definitely one of them. As I talked him through my programme idea, he was going, 'Yah, yah!' and making notes, but he just didn't look that interested.

Mate, I can tell you're not going to make this documentary, I thought to myself. *You're just not.* And I was right, I never heard back from them.

It was very different when I talked to Danny Horan, Fozia Khan and Emma Hardy at Channel 4 about it in 2020. In fact, they commissioned it to be shown during Black History Month in the October, which meant it would be a very quick turnaround for me to pull it off, but I set out to make a programme that really, really needed to be made and was determined to see it come to life.

It was a documentary focusing on how the generation of Black comics who'd come before me – and the generation of Black comics before them – never got the chance to break through to a mainstream audience because they were blocked. Blocked, or just ignored, by the television industry's gatekeepers.

Originally, I wanted to make a three- or four-part series but there wasn't the time or the budget for that! Then I wanted to do an hour and twenty minutes. In the end, I had to settle for fifty-two minutes to tell the story of thirty or forty years of systematic racism, unfairness and ignorance, which wasn't a problem as it meant that the documentary was very intense and focused. Over-all, it added up to a great chance to get the message across and Channel 4 were great in supporting us by allowing the show to be broadcast during a great slot.

But the message *had* to get across.

I didn't want to water it down and make it nice and soft for a TV audience. I wanted to make it raw and make it clear that for many, *many* years, the people commissioning TV entertainment shows should have done a lot, lot better.

I wanted to highlight the Black comedy scene that came before me in Britain and how those talented comics had just never got their dues or the national exposure that they deserved. The comedians like Slim who used to sell out the Hackney Empire weekend after weekend but never got nearly enough TV opportunities.

'If you want to use the word "fuckeries", this is how you would really use it in a sentence,' I said at the beginning of the programme. 'Let's rewind. The time is 1984. Sir Lenny Henry gets his own show. I wasn't even born. I was still in my dad's ball bags.'

'Then fast-forward fifteen years later, to 1999. I was just leaving secondary school. *That* was when Richard Blackwood got to front his own TV show.'

'Then, twenty years later, 2019, the latest show was fronted by myself, Mo Gilligan. That's right! Twenty years before a Black comedian could get a show! And *that* is a "fuckeries" ...'

Working with the brilliant director, Vanessa, I talked to a whole load of great Black comics who have worked the Black comedy circuit for years – people who helped to pave the way for me and my generation – and they all told the same story of beating their heads against the wall.

Quincy, the award-winning comedian who has been selling out venues for fifteen years, said:

'It's treating Black comics like Halley's Comet! "Oh look, there goes one!" "Oh look, there's another one, ten years later!"'

Gina Yashere agreed:

'It was that nightclub policy – one in, one out. They have got one Black person, and that Black person represents all Black people!'

'We're not saying we want everything,' said Kane Brown, who has been on the circuit for over ten years now. 'We just don't want it to be that they give us something for six months, then disappear for the next twenty years! That's not going to be any good for our scene.'

The documentary isn't about Black comedians wanting special treatment, or positive discrimination, or anything like that.

All everybody was saying that they wanted, all they – we – had *ever* wanted, was a level playing field.

'The White artists jump on a train, and it takes them from a panel show to being interviewed by Jonathan Ross, to suddenly it's Christmas and they have a DVD and a book out,' noted Curtis Walker, the Black comic who first came up in the early 1990s on the BBC sketch show *The Real McCoy*.

'They do a journey, from bruck to millionaire after about a year. Well, I'm still bruck! It's fifteen years later and I'm still bruck!'

I thought it was important that *Black, British and Funny* celebrated the scene and the circuit that these comics had established and come up through, rather than solely focusing on the negative aspects. The Black British circuit is a vibrant community full of incredible talent. I knew a lot of people watching the documentary would never have heard of it and would realise that they'd been missing out. I wanted those people to think, *Woah! How did I not know about this!*

Nobody wants to miss out on something. Imagine if I told you that there is a whole world of secret films hidden away on Netflix, and only my friends and me know how to access them? Straight away, you'd be like, *Wow! I want in on this!* And that was how I wanted viewers to feel about this generation of Black comedians that they had missed out on.

Inevitably, some anger came through as well. Mr Cee, who has been a star on the Black circuit for the last twenty years, said, 'People ask me, "When are we gonna see you on TV?" And I say, "You are *never* gonna see me on TV! They're not gonna have it!"'

They're depressing words and they're born out of frustration. I knew that, before this documentary, people like Mr Cee and Kane Brown had never been on primetime TV before. And the picture feels just as bleak on both sides of the cameras.

'The dream I have is producing or directing a sitcom that is full of White people, but behind the cameras, everybody is Black,' admitted Curtis Walker. 'Isn't that a sad dream to have?'

'I think that would scare the hell out of the world! Everybody Black behind the cameras, calling the shots for White actors and comedians! Then we can say to them, "No, I don't think middle Brixton would get it! I don't think middle Handsworth would get it!"'

What Curtis was echoing was 100% true. Because that is what senior TV people thought, and assumed, for years:

Middle England just wouldn't GET Black comedians.

As we talked, we kept coming back to the same people – the commissioning editors. The *gatekeepers*. And Slim, my early hero who had turned me onto stand-up when I had seen him in Deptford all those years ago, summed it up brilliantly.

'That's the fucked-up part!' he said. 'It's the gatekeepers. It's not the audience. I perform to a whole room full of White people and they fucking love it! The [television] audience is being denied our talents – and it's the gatekeepers, I'm telling you!'

• • •

When Black people are excluded from television, it becomes the view of the country that we export to the world. When I went to some parts of America, I discovered that they don't even realise we have a Black British comedy community in the UK.

Well, that's not quite true. We have the likes of Oscar-winning actor Daniel Kaluuya, John Boyega, Damson Idris, Idris Elba and Cynthia Erivo who are currently smashing it in Hollywood. With the other exports like *Top Boy*, which has done amazingly well across the pond, it's proof that young Black Britons are doing well in the US and there are *definitely* Black people in the UK! But they don't know about the Black British comedy scene, and why should they? Nor does mainstream Britain! Like those actors I've mentioned, they've had to go further afield to find success.

Sometimes, Black British comics look to America directly. Gina Yashere was the first comedian from the UK to appear on *Def Comedy Jam*, back in 2008, and since then she has starred on many US stand-up and chat shows, as well as her own scripted projects, including her own Netflix special, which she filmed in LA. She's become a huge star over there.

And what Gina says is true: it *is* one in, one out in this country. When I got given *The Lateish Show*, a lot of people assumed that *The Big Narstie Show* was done. Cancelled. Finished. Finito: 'Ah, Mo, now you've got your own show. Does that mean *The Big Narstie Show* will be cancelled?'

I don't blame them for that: it's the way we've been conditioned to think. But it makes me angry. I was saying, 'No, man, we're *both* gonna have our shows! They're *both* coming back!' But I could see a few people weren't sure whether to believe me. They *wanted* to, but if history had shown us anything, they thought they would probably be right.

Ultimately, I wanted *Black, British and Funny* to say this to our television commissioning editors and executives:

> *What do you want your legacy to be? Do you want to be part*
> *of a channel, or a process, that just commissions bits and bobs*
> *– 'Oh, here's an entertainment show! Here's another one!'*
> *Or do you want to be able to say, 'I made a change and put*
> *people on TV who had never been on before?'*

And the answer is in their hands. In the gatekeepers' hands. It always has been. And it still is.

It would help if there were more people of colour commissioning shows and in senior executive roles at the broadcasters. Right now, the only people I know are June Sarpong at the BBC and Syeda Irtizaali and Becky Cadman at Channel 4. But we need more ...

What was nice was that when *Black, British and Funny* went out as part of Black History Month, it was alongside a whole load of other programmes made by Black production companies. There was a taboo-busting show called *Black Hair*, as well as a programme asking *Is Covid Racist?*

I know Yinka Bokinni, the writer and DJ. Yinka was a school friend and neighbour of Damilola Taylor when he got killed in Peckham in 2000, aged ten, and she went back to their estate to make a documentary about his murder twenty years on. It was an amazing documentary, which went on to win an RTS award.

It was a good spread of programmes during Black History Month because it covered loads of different areas – crime, racism, culture, comedy. And it made me feel as if my documentary was part of something, not just a one-off.

It's funny … I was talking about asking television gatekeepers what they want their legacy to be, and if I ask myself that question, I think I'd like to think that *Black, British and Funny* is a bit of legacy that I leave behind. Because I am *so* pleased that I was able to make that show happen.

I watched the final cut before it went out and I just thought, *Wow! That is a great piece of TV we have made*! I've been lucky enough to make and be involved in the creative process on a load of cool things like my own TV show and the Netflix special, but this was different. *Totally different.*

Why? Because so many talented Black comics got a chance to be on TV who had never been on before. And that was what it was all about.

I'll admit it – I've watched that documentary over and over again. Ten or fifteen times. I think it joins a lot of dots and it is almost like an archive of the story of Black British comedy over the last twenty or thirty years. All captured in a show that's just under an hour long. It is a story that had never been told, but one that deserved to be.

When it came out, people really connected with it. It was trending on Twitter, in a very positive way. A lot of people, comics *and* others, thanked me for doing it and said that it meant so much to them. It was so moving. I mean, I didn't cry – but I was very close!

I believe *Black, British and Funny* is a genuine piece of history and, in the future, I would love it to be shown in schools and universities. I want as many people to see it as possible. I am so, so proud of that television programme.

•   •   •

Why did I set up Momo G Productions? Why did I do it? My thinking went like this: *I want to create stuff for myself, and I want to own the rights to it, and have creative control of how I do it and why I do it. And I want to make it BIGGER!*

I'm not claiming that I've done anything unique. Loads of artists have their own production companies. But given the opportunity, I always big up mine and talk about it whenever I can because to a lot of people, the whole process is shrouded in mystery. They ask me, 'You started your own production company? How do you *do* that?'

And the answer is – it's easy! Anyone can do it. It's just like music producers forming their own record labels. Exactly the same.

That's why, when I was making *The Lateish Show*, something like *Happy Hour* or the Netflix special, I collaborated with people to understand how they do it. Then, eventually, you can start to do it for yourself. It's a learning process. I know some people wanna go it alone right from the start and that's OK too but, for me, working with people and asking for help often got you better results.

I knew instinctively that having my own production company would be important going forward in my career. The team at

Momo G and I have a say in all elements of the productions we do. That voice, my vision and the ideas, has to be heard. That's why I've done it, and I'm so glad that I did.

• • •

I love doing serious projects like *Black, British and Funny* but not everything I've done recently has been so heavyweight. When you're lucky enough to get a little bit well-known, as I have, you get offered all sorts of fun things to do – and one of them was Soccer Aid.

I got to take part in September 2020 at Old Trafford, playing alongside people like Jason Manford, Olly Murs and Joe Wicks. It was sick, although it was a shame COVID-19 meant there was no crowd there.

It's funny because playing that match reminded me of how I wanted to be a footballer at school when I was fourteen, before I discovered Miss Simpson's drama lessons and got into comedy. And, looking back, I didn't have a clue what I was talking about.

I was just playing with my mates and imagining being Ian Wright or Thierry Henry – I had no idea what footballers have to go through to stay at the top. Even if I *had* stuck at it, I don't think it would have worked out for me. You need to be an exceptional talent. Maybe I'd have gone into coaching?

I prefer football being a fun hobby and I wouldn't want to put my body through that much strain. I would much rather do stand-up in front of 10,000 people than play football in front of an audience that large. It sounds like way too much stress!

I captained the Rest of the World team against England, which meant I was the captain of Patrice Evra, Claude Makélélé and Robbie Keane. I also got to share this moment and chill out with friends I know in the industry like Dave, Chunkz and Filly, and Kem Cetinay from *Love Island*. Robbie Keane scored for us, ended up winning on penalties and, in the process, we ended up raising £9 million for UNICEF. It was an experience that I'll never forget.

And, as well as all the other unique opportunities I was being sent, I also got offered another, very fun gig.

• • •

ITV got in touch in early 2020 to say that they liked what I do and would like to have a talk. We chatted about possible ideas and, during the course of the conversation, Katie Rawcliffe, who heads up entertainment for the network, casually asked me, 'What do you think of *The Masked Singer*, Mo?'

As it happened, Joel Dommett was a guest on *The Big Narstie Show*, so I'd watched some clips of him hosting *The Masked Singer* in my pre-interview research. I actually thought it was quite a cool show.

I'd seen Skin, from Skunk Anansie, singing Stormzy's 'Blinded by Your Grace'… dressed as a duck. She did a great version from inside her duck costume, with a whole choir of ducks behind her. I thought to myself, *This is pretty sick!*

I liked how it was just harmless TV. It wasn't like *The X Factor*, where you see people get vilified if they can't sing and it feels like their whole life and future depends on it. Nah, man – it was just people dressing up in funny costumes and singing, which all looked like fun!

A few days after my chat with ITV, I was driving with my girl-friend, getting a takeaway, when Polly called me up.

'OK, I've got some big news, Mo,' she began.

'Yeah? What is it?'

'ITV want you to be a panellist on *The Masked Singer*,' she said.

'Oh my gosh!' This was *totally* out of the blue. I didn't need to think twice about saying yes. Straight away I thought: *I'm TOTALLY going to do Saturday night family TV!*

I felt honoured to be asked! I thought back to being a kid and watching all of those big Saturday night shows like *Gladiators* and *Blind Date*. Not everyone gets to do those huge shows and it felt like it had come at the perfect time in my career.

I like the idea of a young Black boy or girl who doesn't get to stay up to watch *The Lateish Show* or *The Big Narstie Show* watching *The Masked Singer* and seeing someone they can relate to on mainstream Saturday night TV: 'Mum, look at that guy on TV! He looks like dad!' That's got to be good.

Because, for me, that is what it comes down to. I am still representing my community – just on a huge stage.

When it comes down to it, I'm not from a singing back-ground and I'm not holding young people's hopes and dreams in my hands. I'm just sitting there, trying to work out who is singing as a blob, or a sausage. It's family TV and it's fun and it brings everyone together. After the year that a lot of people have had, that's what people needed.

I love being a detective on *The Masked Singer* and trying to work out who is the dragon, or the seahorse, or the grandfather clock. I sometimes sit and look along the line at my fellow judges – Jonathan Ross, Davina McCall, Rita Ora – and I quietly pinch myself.

Am I really here?

I've grown up watching Jonathan Ross and now we're proper friends: I go on his show and he comes on mine. I watched Davina hosting *Big Brother* growing up and now she's coming on my podcast! I was on *The Masked Singer* with them on Boxing Day. *Me, on Boxing Day TV! I couldn't have imagined it.*

It all makes me realise how far I've come, and all I want to do is enjoy it. Enjoy the moment and keep representing my community. And I feel that – I *know* that – I am still doing that.

I tend to do stand-up to people around my age group, but now I'm on primetime TV, it might be their kids who are watching me on telly! *The Masked Singer* viewers might normally watch *The Repair Shop* or *The Great British Bake Off*. I'm bracing myself for young people to start telling me, 'I don't really watch you, Mo, but my mum watches you.'

If I'm going out on tour, I'd love to think that the parents who watch my stuff on TV might buy some tickets and come along. Why not? When Stormzy was selling out the O2, who was buying the tickets? Parents! Get those credit cards out!

•   •   •

By this point my new tour, *There's Mo to Life*, had nearly sold out when, unfortunately, like a lot of live performances it had to be moved to 2021 due to the pandemic. And then I got a call from Polly with another exciting opportunity:

'We've been asked if you'd like to do a show at the O2 Arena in December.'

Hearing those words is quite hard to get your head around. But I couldn't wait to walk out on that stage in front of 20,000 people. The same stage that had seen the likes of Chris Rock, Kevin Hart and Lee Evans. Finally, I was going to have my own headline show at the O2. But in the back of my mind, I didn't want this show to just be about me. I wanted to give this opportunity to those comedians that the gatekeepers wouldn't put on TV and share this exciting moment with them. When the O2 spotlight is shining on me, it's only right that I shine it on others. The comedians that have paved the way for me to achieve mainstream success and the new generation that have come up alongside me.

So instead of doing a one-off show from my tour at the O2, I decided to do a show called *Mo Gilligan and Friends: The Black British Takeover*, which would showcase some of the UK's best Black British comedians who had never performed at the O2 before. People like Slim, my good friend Babatunde and Eddie Kadi.

Once we had got a date finalised, the whole project was very top secret, and gearing up to a big announcement, I'd asked for the help of some of my celebrity friends to tease the news. People such as Daniel Sturridge, Tinie Tempah, Ian Wright and Reggie Yates – just to name a few – recorded videos, for me to upload on my social channels.

That weekend before the announcement, I ended up getting loads of calls from friends asking what the big news that I was teasing on my social media was. But I kept my cards close to my chest and didn't reveal anything. In fact, I spent the whole weekend nervous that some big news outlet would find out what was going on and spill the beans before I could have the chance to.

Luckily, I woke up early on the Monday morning that we were making the announcement. I have a habit of sleeping in on big announcements, but this time I was prepared, with my caption already composed in Notes on my phone, I posted about the biggest announcement of my career to date. When I shared the news on my social channels it went absolutely crazy. Not only were people excited about the prospect of me performing at the O2, they also loved the fact that I was bringing some of the greatest Black comedians along with me to share the experience.

It's one thing announcing the show, it's another being told that you've sold out the O2 Arena, knowing you're going to walk out to a screaming crowd of 20,000 people, who will all be witnessing history. *Mo Gilligan and Friends: The Black British Takeover* will be the first time that a show like this has ever taken place at the O2, a line-up of solely Black British comedians, some of whom have paved the way and laid the foundations for Black British comedy.

• • •

When I look back to when I was young, I didn't really know I was funny, although everyone around me always told me that I was. I was just someone who was laid back and went with the flow.

But my mum has always raised me to be respectful and pursue what I'm passionate about. Comedy has been the thing that has opened so many doors for me. Half the people I know in my life I've met through doing comedy. It's taught me not to give up, it's taught me to ask for help, it's taught me that working in a team is always better than working by yourself. It's allowed me to see the world in ways I never thought I would and to have experiences that money can't buy. Along the way it has been hard, I've had to work very hard to stick at it and stay on course, and like any journey there's always going to be a few diversions along the way, but it's important to also enjoy the journey and trust the process.

It's like what Ian from Live Nation told me when I was sitting in my dressing room backstage during *The Coupla Cans Tour*:

'Enjoy the moment. It's only going to get bigger from here.'

He was absolutely right.

Looking back at it, the journey to where I am today has been one of the most enjoyable parts. It's when success comes along that you have to work harder than ever. When I look back at those times of not having enough money to get the train, it was all worth it. Everything was worth it. I wouldn't change a single part. Every moment has taught me something and has made me come out the other side a better person.

A lot of people always tell me, 'You seem so positive and you're always laughing.' Partly that is because I am living my own dream. Every day I feel like I'm in my own blockbuster film. I don't know what's going to happen tomorrow but every time I think I've reached one height, there's always another level to go.

Just like that rollercoaster: it's not till the ride stops that you realise how fun it was. And just like the rollercoaster, I'm going to keep riding it and see where it takes me. The fun thing about this rollercoaster, though, is that everyone gets to come along for the ride. So, if you're reading this: don't stop and never give up.

PICTURE CREDITS

Section one: all author's private collection.

Section two: all author's private collection except p. 1 bottom © David M. Benett / Getty; p. 2 bottom © Mykool Thomas; p. 3 middle and bottom © Mykool Thomas; p. 4 middle © Guy Levy/ BAFTA/ Shutterstock, bottom © David M. Benett/Getty; p. 5 top, middle and bottom © The Lateish Show With Mo Gilligan/Channel 4/Expectation Entertainment Limited, p. 6 top and bottom © David Geli; p. 7 top © Jonny Birch/BAFTA/ Shutterstock, bottom © David Geli; p. 8 bottom © Mykool Thomas.